TITANIC POETRY, MUSIC & STORIES

KEN ROSSIGNOL

KEN ROSSIGNOL

DEDICATION

To Brooks, Charlie, Grace & Aubrey

.

CONTENTS

ACKNOWLEDGMENTS

The Library of Congress, the Maritime Museum of the Atlantic, the National Museum of Northern Ireland, the British Library, The Library of Virginia, the Chicago Museum of Technology, the New York Public Library, the photos of Fr. Francis Browne, Bain News Service, The New York Times, The New York Herald, The World, The Washington Times, The Richmond Times Dispatch

The Titanic
Song & words by Mrs. N. M. Sanders ; music by M. C. Hanford. 1912

First line:
When the great ship Titanic on her maiden trip sailed for home she took one thousand noble hearts on board who met their doom.
Refrain:
The Titanic she went under, the Titanic met her doom..

Introduction

Many great accounts of the fateful night of April 14th and 15th of 1912 have been told about the sinking of the *RMS Titanic*. Over the past one hundred and one years, the stories of the people and the disaster have been explained in art, movies, books, music and verse.

This book begins with an original poem I have written to commemorate the ship's first, last and only voyage and the heroics demonstrated by some of those souls on board, some who survived and others who did not.

Other wonderful and historic poems from the years immediately following the disaster are included here along with musical tributes, some of which can be linked to hear historic renditions on ebooks and computers.

Some of the poems are famous, while others were penned by unknown poets.

Newspapers of the day found that they received unsolicited poems by the hundreds on a daily basis - so many that the editor of the *New York Times* penned an editorial declaring many to be unworthy. The editorial concluded with a harsh admonition to its readers that simply because one had pen and paper didn't anoint them with the talent of a poet. Newspapers of today tend to be considerably friendlier to their declining readerships.

What all those who wrote the poems of the *Titanic* shared in common was the desire of those authors to express shock, despair and sorrow in all the depths of human emotion. In addition, the very best attributes of character, heroics and courage were described in verse and song as exhibited or even imagined to have been displayed by the valiant on board the *Titanic.*

Included here are two original poems penned by me along with my favorite story about the hero dog of the Titanic, Rigel, which I tell to visitors at the Titanic Museums in Pigeon Forge, Tennessee and Branson, Missouri, where I hope to see you when you visit. — **Ken Rossignol**

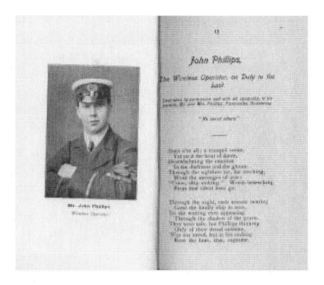

Jack Phillips, one of the heroes of the Titanic, used every available second of the two hours and forty minutes prior to the sinking of the ship, to send S.O.S. and C.Q.D. messages to other ships at sea, before he dove into the dark and cold water in an attempt to save his own life. Phillips could have also been blamed for the sinking of the ship as the most recent warning of ice ahead to be transmitted to the Titanic, was received by Phillips, who failed to deliver it to the bridge. At 9:30 pm, the *Mesaba* sent a stark warning to the Titanic that ice was directly ahead. Phillips kept the message at his desk and continued to transmit routine messages to Cape Race. Assistant wireless operator Harold Bride reported later that he saw Phillip's body as he boarded the Carpathia when they were rescued.

The Story of the Titanic

By Ken Rossignol

From across the Old World they came to cross the sea,

On the shiny new liner of White Star line and soon filled most every cabin to answer the plea,

Of how to leave famine, misery and sickness behind and travel to the New World; to follow their destiny.

Some were wealthy, and others were accomplished and talented in the arts and letters,

While fifty of the best waiters in London were chosen to serve their wealthy betters.

From crew to officers and dandies too, there were gamblers, journalists and con-men as well,

Even two lads stolen from their mother by their father were on board to hear the last bell.

For four days a roar of fire deep in the coal bunkers was fought,

As the crew worked round the clock, all for naught.

Above decks, all was well and Father Browne left in Queenstown with his camera full of the only photo history of the trip,

And the lookouts left with too with the binoculars of the mighty ship.

The warnings came from all over the sea lanes that fearsome ice lay ahead,

But Captain Smith ignored all the reports of bergs, a decision he would soon dread.

High on the crow's nest, Frederick Fleet called down the warning, not once, not twice but three times he pleaded,

On the bridge, First Officer Mr. Murdock never heeded.

Only when it was too late did he give the order to change course,

To find that the ship would soon collide with a giant berg with great force.

The captain ordered the wireless men
to send out calls by SOS,

To summon the assistance of all ships at
sea of their great distress.

From millionaires to stewards, there
were few willing to leave in haste,

As no one would believe such a great
ship would have a berg make it waste.

Soon the ship dipped towards the bow,

As the wails of those left behind by
lifeboats began a mournful howl.

The *Carpathia* began its mission of
salvation across the dark sea,

While the *Californian* slumbered closer
unaware of the urgency.

Alexander's Ragtime Band, Autumn and
Nearer My God to Thee,

Were played by the brave eight in the
band led by Wallace Hartley.

Brave men assisted women and children
into the boats,

While cowards plotted ways to keep
afloat.

Boilers exploded, shots rang out,
rockets were fired and many expired,

As the *Titanic* began its descent and the first began to slip below the surface as their bodied tired.

Postal clerks from both sides of the Atlantic,

Led by Oscar Scott Woody, they worked furiously to save the mail from the mighty *Titanic.*

Women looked on from lifeboats as the men they left behind stood at the ship's rail,

Their screams at seeing their fathers, sons and husbands last moments caused most to wail,

"Be British" Capt. Smith told his crew in his last words and Maj. Butt asked a woman to remember him to the folks back home,

As he made sure she was comfortable and warm in the lifeboat in which he was not to roam.

One brave woman found she was soon in command of all in her boat,

As she only had three men, one too old, another too frozen and the other a coward who only sang a sour note.

"We will all die," he said for we have no water, no lantern and no bread,

"Quiet, you fool, they are coming for us, I know, because the wireless man told me so and if you don't shut up I will smack you with an oar right in your lame head!"

Then the women in the boat began to moan, to cry and to despair,

And who could blame them for they lost their loved ones and had ice in their hair.

The women told her they didn't know which way to row and we will likely all drown,

She told them to shut up and row as that would keep them warm and forever after that night she was known as the Unsinkable Molly Brown.

For three hours the air was still, the ocean was dead calm - as the heavens began to retrieve the souls that fluttered along,

Soon the *Carpathia* was seen in the early morning mist and the survivors broke into song.

Hot soup, coffee and hot chocolate awaited them on the wonderful ship of the Cunard line,

And passengers of the *Carpathia* gave the survivors warm clothes, their cabins as they knew they were in a bind.

One woman tried to console her young daughter over the loss of her favorite toy,

And feared having to explain how her father had perished as had their boy.

In time the lessons of not enough lifeboats for all,

Were borne out in hearings the Senate would call.

The fire weakened the hull at the critical point the ship hit the ice,

Leaving most of those onboard without a chance at a longer life.

Milvina Dean was but a tot who's Pop stuffed her in a mail sack,

And she lived to be the last survivor alive in 2009 with her name on a plaque.

The chairman of the White Star line escaped from ship, his name was Bruce Ismay,

And his explanations of why he failed to provide enough lifeboats were met with dismay.

As the great liners race across the railless tracks of the sea,

The story of the *RMS Titanic* will live on into infamy.

Oscar Scott Woody, one of five postal clerks on the *Titanic*. He was from North Carolina and his salary was $1,000 a year. All five died trying to save the mail on the sinking ship.

POEM ON TITANIC BAND STIRRED NEW YORK SOCIETY.

The New York Herald

New York City, May 14, 1912 --- As a memorial to the band of the Titanic, which played as the ship sank; Miss Amy Baker yesterday afternoon recited a poem

called "*The Band That Played Till the Ship Went Down*."
It was written by Miss Mary Moffat Cunningham, of this
city, and was one of many selections by Miss Baker at
her annual recital in Rumford Hall.

The recitation brought tears to the eyes of many in
the audience. It was:

The Band That Played Till the Ship Went Down

By Mary Moffat Cunningham

What were the thoughts of the band who stood
Waiting the word of command?
Not a man of them showed surprise.
Did they know? Were they told?
Were the timid made bold
By the look in their leader's eyes?
Knitting his brow with a puzzled frown,
Calmly he lifted his hand: -
"Attention, please! Are you ready?
Good!
Then play like men till the ship goes down!
Play for the husbands who part from wives,
Play for the brave who give up their lives!
'Tis the strong for the weak.
Make the instruments speak!
Now play like men till the ship goes down!
Play for the fleet of drifting boats,
Play for the widows in distress,
Play for the children fatherless!
Oh, hark! Did you hear
That ghost of a cheer?

How far away the music floats!
Play on, brave lads, till the ship goes down.
Give them a waltz, now, a rollicking rag!
Play for the pride of the English flag.
(That girl I love In Yorkshire town,)
Play on, good boys, play on!
(Her lips are sweet, and her eyes are brown,
So fair to look upon)!
Play on, my men, till the ship goes down!
(Easy I'm told for a man to drown),
Some cursing luck, some on their knee.
Who's speaking there? One moment, please!
We're sinking fast. The lights grow dim.
A woman here who wants a hymn.
How does it run? By woes to be -
Nearer, My God- to Thee- to Thee,'
(Good bye, dear girl, good bye,
 I'm not afraid to die).
God of the dark, God of the sea,
Through night to light, we come to Thee!
Well, boys! we've played our best,
Now leave to God the rest.
We die like men when the ship goes down!"

The Unsinkable Molly Brown

By Ken Rossignol

A hard-working woman and her husband had hit it big deep in the mountains of Colorado as they dug for gold,
Their efforts allowed for them both to seek an easier life and she chose to take a trip to the world of old.

From Rome to London and then to the
wonders of Paris, France,
Margaret Brown found her mind enriched, the
art enthralled her with a trance.
After gathering all the culture that could be
swept up in her breast,
Margaret knew it was time to be on her way to
Denver and rest.

She booked a trip back across the sea on the
newly-minted Titanic,
Not knowing that life would soon be a panic.
The days passed pleasantly as the great ship
stopped in several ports,
And the evenings offered more occasions for
learning of sorts.

Late in the evening of the fourth day, a great
berg stood in the ship's way,
A crash and a gash would soon put the ship
asunder,
As explosions and rockets startled the night
like thunder.

Margaret Brown's fate was to be cast off in a
lifeboat
As the mighty Titanic struggled to stay afloat.
In the dark of night without lamp or light,
Mrs. Brown took a look at those with whom
she was cast off in the night.

Of only three men on board, she later wrote,
one was useless as he was too old,
While another man was frozen and could not
row due to the cold.
That left only a third man of the several dozen
souls and soon her spirit quickly soured,
When she realized the last man was simply a
coward!

He railed and ranted as he declared that they
had no food or water and would soon die!
Mrs. Brown looked hard at the man and
squinted her eye,
And promised him that he kept up his moaning
and groaning she would make sure he would
quickly find a speedy trip to the ocean floor,
As she was perfectly capable of bashing him in
the head with an oar!

Margaret Brown then had to deal with more
than two dozen women who were all in a fright,
For they had left all their men behind to die on
that terrible night!
Brown told them to make up for the lack of
men and for each to help row,
But they cried, they sobbed and threw up their
hands with no destination that of they know.

"It matters not where we row, for the wireless man told me that help was on the way, as he is the one who heard the call answer his SOS."
"I know there will be help here soon to quell your distress."
"We will row to stay warm and this will make you live," said Brown,
"Now everyone take a turn and we sing and pray with a great sound."

Margaret put them all to the task, with one woman to lift the oar and the other to pull,
They lasted the night until daybreak revealed the rescue ship Carpathia and that the coward had indeed been a fool.
The women rejoiced at their salvation and soon were given food and warmth of the rescuers that they found,
And forever more, Margaret was known as the Unsinkable Molly Brown!

The Titanic
By Brand Whitlock

Collier's – The National Weekly, June 15, 1912

"And This," the dark Ironic Spirit mocked
As it beheld the proud new lofty ship
Upon its westering way across the sea,
"This is thy latest, greatest miracle,
The triumph of thy science, art and all
That skill thou'st learnt since forth the Norsemen fared
Across these waters in their cockle shells,
In dodging back and forth 'twist storm and sea,
Until at last, in this they master work,
Thou does go in safety and in pride, and boast
Meanwhile of thine unparalleled achievement,
Thy victory o'er my wanton will and whim!
Ho, Little Man, behold! I'd not waste e'en
A tempest on thy paragon, but thus,
Upon its first glad, confident adventure,
With but a cast-off fragment of my store
Of power--thus to the bottom of the seas
For evermore, with thy latest marvel
And with thee! Ho! Ho!
The awful laugh
Rang through the dreadful reaches of the Void.
But lo! The calm and all-sufficient answer
Of our intrepid Northern race! With lips
Drawn tight, they look with clear, dry eyes on doom,
And so confront the end, there in the night
That was to have for them no pitying dawn.

(Their kind alone of all intelligence
Feels pit.)
"The women and the children first.
We stay."
No cry, no whimpering; and there,
Up there upon the dark, mysterious bridge,
The grizzled captain, chief of all those victims
Of its sublime, stupendous, bitter joke,
But the exemplar of that race which knows
How to aspire, achieve, and dare Its wrath,
And in the hour of failure, how to die.

No Icebergs in Heaven?

One of the hundred or more poems about the Titanic disaster, received by *The Star*, voices the refrain that there are "no icebergs in Heaven." It may be suggested that there are no icebergs in the Other Place, either.

--- Kansas City Star.

The best Titanic poem I have seen is William Hardy's, read In London the other day in the presence of the King. Here is the concluding verse

In the solitude of the sea,'
Deep from human vanity.
And the pride of life that planned her, stilly couches she
Over the mirrors meant
To flash forms opulent,
The sea-worm creeps grotesque, unwitting, mean, content.

CHILD WRITES POEM ON TITANIC FOR CIRCLE

Seattle Star

May 4, 1912 Seattle, Washington

---Dear Uncle Jack: I am a girl, 13 years old and am sending you a poem I wrote about the Titanic disaster. May I please join your circle? I am a Seattle girl, although I live in Havelyon, Cal.

Yours truly,

CHRYSTAL MOHR.

TITANIC

By Chrystal Mohr

Oh' Titanic, monster of the sea

All is rest and peace with thee.

The sun may shine, the rain may rain,

But on your decks never again

Will the sound of children sweet.

'Twas on a fatal Sunday night.

When all was calm and your lights were shining bright,

All of a sudden there was a crash, a cry, 'tis all too late,

For thou, oh, great Titanic, has met thy fate.

Boats were made ready.

The men were strong and steady,

The women and children dangers must face,

While the men go to their last resting place.

Amid the encircling gloom,

The brave men must go to their doom '

The Carpathia, a ship so strong.

Did not take long
To reach the ill-fated boat.
But alas, she was not afloat.
Now this all happened on a Sunday night,
When all was calm and your lights were bright
The sun may shine, the rain may rain,
But feet will never tread the Titanic decks again.

This famous photo taken by Father Frank Browne, who left the ship in Ireland, shows a boy playing on the deck of the ship. He survived, as did his father next to him but tragically, both died within a few years, the boy drowned in a swimming pool and the father in an auto crash.

San Juan Islander
Friday Harbor, Washington – April 26, 1912
The day after the Titanic disaster the following appeared in the Seattle Post Intelligencer, written by Tom Dillon, a member of the paper's editorial staff. It immediately attracted wide attention, and was reprinted in the Sunday P. I by request:

Fate's Comedy

By Tom Dillon

A thousand years since Fate had planned
To stage a playlet on the sea;
And moved her pawns with patient hand
To build a merry comedy.

She caught the rain drops from. the sky
And welded them with icy blows,
Until they towered mountain high,
An iceberg mid the Northland floes.

A thousand years have come and gone,
While men have slowly learned their part;
Each gave his little brain or brawn,
That Fate might try her comic art.

Some burrowed deep in endless night,
To break the steel from earth's strong grip,
While others forged the atoms bright
And built for Fate a noble ship.

They pitted toil and ant-like skill
Against the chance of Fate's grim game;
With hope to fright her cruel will,
They gave their craft a giant's name. ;

And when the scene-and stage were set,
And all things tuned in time and space,
The puppet ship and iceberg met,
True in the long appointed place.

A little crash that scarce was heard
Across the pulsing deep a mile,
A little cry, a frightened word,
And Fate put on an age-worn smile.

The stars looked down in cold content,
The waves rolled on their endless way,
And jaded Fate, her interest spent, V
Began to plot another play.

Getting the news at the White Star line office in New York.

THE GREATEST WRECK IN THE WORLD'S MARITIME HISTORY—THE LOSS OF THE "TITANIC"

This supreme act of snobbery appeared in the *New York Times* after the newspaper was inundated with poems about the Titanic disaster:

Only Poets Should Write Verse

"In spite of our gentle hint, the other day, that more people were sending to this office verses on the Titanic than were qualified as poets worthily to treat a subject so large and difficult, the flood of these contributions continues.

No longer, indeed, are we getting a hundred or so a day, but they are still coming in by the dozen, and though they all get a reading as patient as circumstances will permit, it does seem time to say again that to write about the Titanic a poem worth printing requires that the author should have something more than paper, pencil and a strong feeling that the disaster was a terrible one.

Ignorance of that fact, or failure to remember it, has caused many worthy and well-intentioned people to ask – often with pathetic confidence – the publication of verses which, had the request been granted, would have caused cruel humiliation for the authors. For it is no exaggeration to say that a large majority of these offerings have been worthless, and that not a few, judged by any standards of literature and taste, have been intolerably bad. Many of them had not the subject been so serious, would have been..."

Only Poets Should Write Verse. In spite of our gentle hint, the other day, that more people were sending to this office verses on the Titanic than were qualified as poets worthily to treat a subject so large and difficult, the flood of these contributions continues. No longer, indeed, are we getting a hundred or so a day, but they are still coming in by the dozen, and though they all get a reading as patient as circumstances will permit, it does seem time to say again that to write about the Titanic a poem worth printing requires that the author should have something more than paper, pencil, and a strong feeling that the disaster was a terrible one.

Ignorance of that fact, or failure to remember it, has caused many worthy and well-intentioned people to ask—often with pathetic confidence—the publication of verses which, had the request been granted, would have caused cruel humiliation for the authors. For it is no exaggeration to say that a large majority of these offerings have been worthless, and that not a few, judged by any standards of literature and taste, have been intolerably bad. Many of them, had not the subject been so serious, would have been

WHITE STAR LINE.

YOUR ATTENTION IS SPECIALLY DIRECTED TO THE CONDITIONS OF TRANSPORTATION IN THE ENCLOSED CONTRACT.

THE COMPANY'S LIABILITY FOR BAGGAGE IS STRICTLY LIMITED, BUT PASSENGERS CAN PROTECT THEMSELVES BY INSURANCE.

First Class Passenger Ticket per Steamship

SAILING FROM

This is a first class passenger ticket for the Titanic.

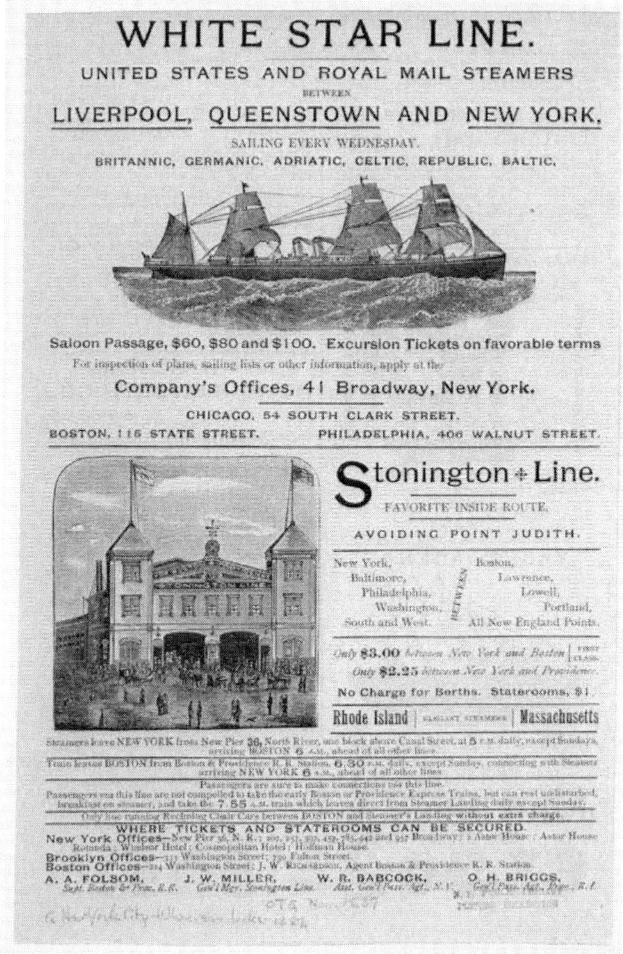

THE SINKING OF THE TITANIC

By C. Victor Stahl (1915)

Oh, Titan was her gorgeous armament
    And Titan was her sail and crew;
A thing of pride to sweep the surging tide
    And laugh to scorn the perilous blue.
Yet let us weep not for her treasured hulk
    That sank leagues deep into the sea,
But for the toll of ill-starred voyagers
    Who rode her to eternity.

I see the glory of that primal hour
    When first her beams did breast the wave,
Yea, owner, builder, seaman's eyes did sparkle
    As did the sea her huge side lave: —
How zealously the elite madly rushed
    To trust their passage in her care,
To boast their presence on the maiden trip
    Of that leviathan so rare.

She sailed. — The sky gleamed bright and
    azure clear.
    The waves lashed gently at her side.
The moon that night shone down auspiciously
    Upon that ship of gorgeous pride.
Her engines tore in frenzy o'er and o'er.
    Her powerful shafts did heave and quake.
As loud and clear her captain's voice rang out,
    "Speed on! Fear not the iceberg's brake."

Ahead there floundered in the chilly sea
    A huge and bristling wall of ice.
"What shall we do?" her helmsman tremulously
cried.
      Word came, "Let's cleave it in a trice,"
    Whereat the mighty engines creaked and strained
      And madly sped the Titan hulk.
    Ne'er moved nor stirred the ocean's icy berg.
      But braced against her speeding bulk.

"Dost thou defy me, master of the sea.
      Thou untried artifice of man?
I'll show thee, then, whose is the stronger hand,
For mine was here e'er thine began."
    Crash! Crash! The waters rushed. The ship's side
heaved.
    The ponderous engines ceased to throb.
And there above the darkening drawbridge cried
    A thousand souls in fear to God.

From peaceful slumbers wildly they up-rose.
      From games of whist, from dance and wine.
    "Can it be so?" they cried in anguished pride —
      "So sinking in the icy brine?"
But ah! alas! the hand of death hung o'er.
      Alas for captain, ship and crew!

    In headstrong haste they'd left the boats behind
    That save men from the watery blue.
    "Let there be women saved, and they alone!"
      Rose up like steel the chivalrous cry,
    While gallant men stood on the slippery deck

And brave resolved themselves to die.
Then solemn strains rose from the engulfing main,
    "Nearer my God," they sang, "to Thee,"
Till all that was left of the Titan's envied hulk
    Was a billowy gurgle in the sea.

Alas for man! Alas for vaunting boast!
    Which seeks to conquer the fate of the sea,
Essays to raise proud hulks of iron and steel
    And laugh to scorn God's mastery!
Thus from their watery grave he lifts his voice ;
    "None tempt my power by craft malign.
Lo! all shall cleave unto the common end.
    And none shall stand but I, divine!"

The famous journalist W. T. Stead wrote years before he died on the *Titanic* that he dreamt he would die in a great calamity.

The Titanic

Harper's Weekly, April 20, 1912
WITHIN the dungeon of the deep
There sleeps the queen of all the seas,

Who swung assurance at the sweep
Of ghostly peril on the breeze,
And dared the elements to ply
Their angered forces at her head
That she might battle and defy –
And lo! One battle left her dead!

With all the graces of a court
She slipped the tethers of the tide
And glided far from out the port
That bound her power and her pride,
And with the promise of her youth
And all the future in her sway,
She strode in triumph over truth
And tossed the danger with the spray1

Within her heart was great and gay,
Without, her sinews stretched in length,
The very heavens seemed to play
Beside the pulses of her strength!
And through the day and through the night
Of billowed pleasure undismayed,
Her throb of fervor set to flight
The toll of fear, and fear obeyed.

Peace! While the even waters glide
By quite stars from night to day;
Peace! While the measured hours stride
In swift descent upon their prey;
And there in shrouded silence steals
The stealthy espion of the sea,
Whose frozen mask afar conceals
The dark decree of destiny.

Peace! While the miracle of man
Yet flies her flag in majesty;
Peace! While she breathes her final span
Serene until eternity;
And then - the muffled knell of doom,
The flash of fate, the riven rod,
The plunge into the gulf of gloom,
And last – the very touch of God!

A thousand lives embosomed are
Beneath the wonders of the wave,
A thousand spirits vanished far
Beyond the waters of the grave;
And sunken in that solemn keep,
The carcass of a vessel vast,
Where only weeds and fishes creep
Among the port-holes of the past!

No marble monolith may mark,
Brave sons! The traces of your doom,
Where but the caverns of the shark
Return the echoes of the tomb,
And but a broken bulk of steel
Crushed in the sea's eternal bed,
Shall tell the distant ages still
Where tender homage may be led.

And yet, about that shattered shell
Whose glory crumbled in an hour,
The waves may wind a coral spell
And weave a poem into power,
Until the heaving depths of slime
And clinging beauties of the deep

Shall mold a monument sublime
Unto your ceremented sleep.

And here, since every sorrow swings
Some note of beauty on the tide,
And not a dark despair but brings
A feeble glimmer to abide,
Bereaved, benumbed, all hearts may fold
About the courage of the dead,
And honor strength that died enrolled
To yield the weaker, life instead.

And while the winds and waters merge
In mournful requiem of sighs,
And chant a great eternal dirge
Of far regret unto the skies,
The wave of all the ages still
Shall sweep the reef of memory,
And yearning breakers curve and thrill
In music of your eulogy!

M. C. Lehr

The Convergence of the Twain

BY **THOMAS HARDY**

1840–1928 Thomas Hardy

(Lines on the loss of the "Titanic")

I
In a solitude of the sea
Deep from human vanity,
And the Pride of Life that planned her, stilly
couches she.

II
Steel chambers, late the pyres
Of her salamandrine fires,
Cold currents thrid, and turn to rhythmic tidal
lyres.

III
Over the mirrors meant
To glass the opulent
The sea-worm crawls — grotesque, slimed,
dumb, indifferent.

IV
Jewels in joy designed
To ravish the sensuous mind
Lie lightless, all their sparkles bleared and
black and blind.

V
Dim moon-eyed fishes near
Gaze at the gilded gear

And query: "What does this vain-gloriousness down here?" ...

VI
Well: while was fashioning
This creature of cleaving wing,
The Immanent Will that stirs and urges everything

VII
Prepared a sinister mate
For her — so gaily great —
A Shape of Ice, for the time far and dissociate.

VIII
And as the smart ship grew
In stature, grace, and hue,
In shadowy silent distance grew the Iceberg too.

IX
Alien they seemed to be;
No mortal eye could see
The intimate welding of their later history,

X
Or sign that they were bent
By paths coincident
On being anon twin halves of one august event,

XI
Till the Spinner of the Years
Said "Now!" And each one hears,
And consummation comes, and jars two hemispheres.

Supplement to The Sphere, April 27, 1912]   THE SPHERE   iii

TERED THE LUXURY OF THE "TITANIC."

THE READING AND WRITING ROOM ON BOARD THE "TITANIC" NOW IN THE DEPTHS OF THE ATLANTIC

The size and equipment of the *Titanic* was such that it was not easy for the minds of the passengers to quickly realise that the warm, beautiful rooms in which they had been spending a pleasant evening or the calm in which they were enjoying the first hour of deep would soon be sinking beneath them. Everything was at first quite leisurely. Colonel Gracie says that when the vessel struck "the passengers were not alarmed, but joked over the matter. The few who appeared on deck had

SUMBER OF PERSONS RESCUED FROM THE "TITANIC"	
First class	202
Second class	115
Third class	178
Crew	206
Officers	4
Total number of saved	705
Number of persons who lost their lives	1,635

taken time to dress properly." Several of the male survivors were in the smoking-room at the time of the contact with the berg. It was probably the fullest public room at the moment. There would also probably have been one or two quiet readers sitting in the room shown above, scanning the pages of a novel before turning in. There had been music and singing during the evening. There were then 2,340 persons on board; of these no fewer than 1,635 perished.

The Harvest of the Sea

By Charles Hanson Towne:

(On the sinking of the Titanic)
The jealous Sea moaned in the April night:
'Lo! there are comrades hidden in my heart,
Unfortunates who sought me, sick of life.
But I am hungry for brave souls; I crave
Their warmth and passion through my chilling
tides;
Their heads upon my bosom, and their hands,
Like children's hands, about me in the dark.
I need their blood in my cold loneliness.'

A Titan sailed her weary leagues of foam,
Unknowing her strange wish, her mad desire.
But there was menace in the starlit night,
And sudden doom upon deceiving paths,
And a wild horror on the mighty deep.

The grey Sea laughed--and drew those brave men
down,
And braver women who but mocked at Death,
Seeing that Love went with them. These the souls
The awful Sea desired! These the hearts
She waited for in that stupendous hour!
They were enough to warm the Arctic wastes,
To fill with furnace heat the frozen zones,
And fire the very Sea that was their grave,
But dream not, mighty Ocean, they are yours!
We have them still, those high and valiant men
Who died that others might reach ports of peace.

Not in your jealous depths their spirits roam,
But though the world today, and up to heaven!

The Titanic Disaster

By J. H. McKenzie

Guthrie, Oklahoma

I.

On the cold and dark Atlantic,
The night was growing late
Steamed the maiden ship *Titanic*
Crowded with human freight
She was valued at Ten Million,
The grandest ever roamed the seas,
Fitted complete to swim the ocean
When the rolling billows freeze.

II

She bade farewell to England
All dressed in robes of white
Going out to plow the briny deep,.
And was on her western flight;
She was now so swiftly gliding
In L Fifty and Fourteen
When the watchman viewed the monster
Just a mile from it, 'Twas seen.

III.

Warned by a German vessel
Of an enemy just ahead
Of an Iceberg, that sea monster,
That which the seamen dread.
On steamed this great *Titanic:*
She was in her swiftest flight;

She was trying to break the record.
On that fearful, fearful night.

IV.

Oh ; she was plowing the Ocean
For speed not known before,
But alas, she struck asunder
To last forever more,
A wireless message began to spread
Throughout the mighty deep, it said,
"We have struck an iceberg, being delayed;
Please rush to us with aid."

V.

The Captain, of the White Star Line,
Who stood there in command,
Was an Admiral of seasoned mind
Enroute to the western land.
The Captain thought not of his life
But stood there to the last
And swimming saved a little child
As it came floating past.

VI.

Outstretched hands offered reward
For his brave and heroic deed
But the intrepid man went down aboard
Trying to rescue a passenger instead
This ill-starred giant of the sea
Was carried to his grave
On the last and greatest ship, was he,
That ever cleft a wave.

VII.

Gay was the crew aboard this ship.
Passengers large and small;
They viewed the coming danger,
They felt it one and all.
On played the grand Orchestra
Their notes were soft and clear;
They realized God's power on land
On sea 'twas just as near.

VIII

So they played this glorious anthem
Continued on the sea
And repeated the beautiful chorus
"Nearer My God To Thee."
Then silenced when the ship went down
Their notes were heard no more.
Surely they'll wear a starry crown
On that Celestial Shore.

IX.

Colonel Astor, a millionaire,
Scholarly and profound,
Said to his wife, "I'll meet you dear
Tomorrow in York Town."
His bride asked a seaman true
"Oh say! may husband go;"
The echo came upon the blue
He answered, "He may, you know."

X.

This man rushed not to his seat
He seemed to have no fear.

Being calm, serene and discreet
Tendered it to a lady near,
"Oh go, he said, mv darling wife
Please be not in despair.
Be of good cheer, as sure as life,
I'll meet you over there."

XI.

Well could he have known this dreadful night
The sea would be his grave
Though he worked with all his might
For those whom he could save.
This man a soldier once has been
Of military art,
Proved himself full competent then
To do his noble part.

XII.

Major Butt, well known to fame
A lady did entreat,
To kindly name him to his friends
Whom she perchance to meet.
He forced the men to realize
The weaker they should save;
He gave his life with no surprise
To the sea — a watery grave;
And with a smile upon his face
He turned to meet his fate,
Soon, soon the sea would be his grave
In and ever after date.

XIII.

And Strauss, who did the children feed,

Had mercy on the poor,
And all such men the world doth need
To reverence evermore.
Oh, may the union of Strauss and wife
Be memorial to all men,
Each for the other gave their life,
A life we should commend;
And may all girls who chance in life
To read this poem thru
Emulate the deed of such a wife,
As went down in the blue.

XIV

Down, down goes the great *Titanic*
With faster and faster speed
Until Alas! there comes a burst
She bade farewell indeed
Farewell, farewell to land and seas,
Farewell to wharves and shore,
For I must land beneath the breeze
To reach the land no more
I carry with me more human weight
Than ever recorded before
To leave them on a land sedate
They will land, Oh! land no more.

XV.

Only a few you see.
May tell the story
Of this great calamity;
Husbands, Wives, perhaps in glory
View the sad catastrophe.
The Carpathia eastern bound

For the Mediterranean Sea,
Turned to the mighty sound,
The wireless C. Q. D.

XVI.

Quick was the preparation made,
To warn the unfortunate few,
For the homeless was cold and delayed
Being chilled by the wind as it blew.
So to the youth
Through life has started,
Be ever thoughtful and true,
Stay by the truth, be not departed
Success shall come to you
Oh, may you shun the Iceberg,
By the dreadful work was wrought,
And prosper by the lesson
This mighty ship has taught.

The Author's Introduction.

I have written these verses, knowing from long experience that in times of great emotion there are many people who like to read of sad events, especially in the medium of metrical language, and such work in rhyme is often more valued, but the "popular reader" in the houses of the people, than the best prose description, and many readers, not too critical, will keep a small book like this when eloquent press-records are put aside.

In addition, most of those who have had copies of these verses, have desired to see these "Records in Rhyme" in book-form to keep in memory of the saddest of sea tragedies.

I claim no poetic power in these verses, so that critics, on the look-out for master-pieces will not find them here, but with a rather wide personal knowledge of "the people' I beg to say that the clear, easily comprehended "rhyme" is generally more treasured by "the masses" than sonnets that may be immortal, but are for the "the few".

EDWIN DREW, London, May 1912.

(This introduction was prepared by Edwin Drew and enclosed with a batch of poems *The Chief Incidents of the 'Titanic' Wreck, Treated in Verse,* he sent to President William Howard Taft and which now is on display at the Library of Congress in Washington, D.C.)

SECTION TWO – THE MUSIC

"The destruction of the Titanic, or the watery grave."

"Man, you are no match for the cold ocean's power. It is a wet and deep grave. Shed tears for all the lives lost. And for her noble courage, all should honor and remember the name of Ida Straus."

Source: Heskes, Irene, Yiddish American Popular Songs, 1895-1950

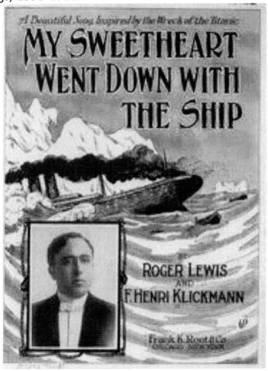

My Sweetheart Went Down With The Ship

For voice and piano.

"A beautiful song, inspired by the wreck of the Titanic." words by Roger Lewis ; music by F. Henri Klickmann.

First line: **Out of the bay sailing away there went the steamship Titanic.**

Refrain: **My sweetheart went down with the ship**. Advertisement for The wreck of the Titanic by Jeanette Forrest on p. 2 and for I will love you when the silver threads are shining among the gold by F. Henri Klickmann on p. [6].

Destruction of the Titanic Words by C. H. Dutton ; music by Etta B. Server. Notes; For voice and piano.

First line: **Beyond the sea from an English harbor.**

Refrain: **While the lifeboats onward moving**.

Advertisement for The mourning turtle dove by M. Hanford on p. [6].

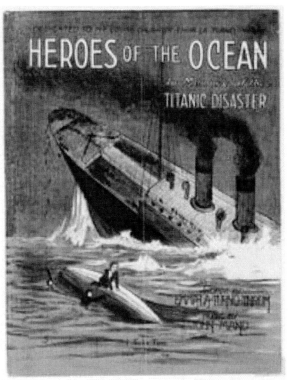

Heroes of the ocean: in memory of the Titanic disaster
For voice and piano. words by Emma La Turno Thrum ;
music by John Mand. Denver, Colorado, 1912
First line: The bright silv'ry moon rose high in the sky.
Refrain: Men kissed their wives and children goodbye.

For voice and piano. Caption title. words and air by
Laura Smith Roush ; arr. by D. L. Roush. Topeka, Kansas,
1912

First line: **Upon the ocean's mighty billows.**
Refrain: **We are sinking, came the wireless.**

Titanic: in the shadows of the deep.

Composer: Held, Wm. Lyricist: Boland, John, lyricist
Place of Publication/Creation: Corry, Pa., 1912
For voice and piano.
First line: **A ship they named the Titanic.**
Refrain: **Good-bye to all dearer than life.**

Autumn (Episcopalian hymn played by the Titanic band as the ship went down, along with Nearer My God to Thee & various ragtime tunes)
http://www.loc.gov/jukebox/recordings/detail/id/2700
     Nearer My God to Thee (performed by Conway's Band, 1915
     http://www.loc.gov/jukebox/recordings/detail/id/4038

Nearer My God to Thee, performed by famous tenor John McCormack in 1913
http://www.loc.gov/jukebox/recordings/detail/id/3265

The Ragtime Drummer by Arthur Pryor's Band was recorded the day after the Titanic left Southampton on April 11, 1912
http://www.loc.gov/jukebox/recordings/detail/id/6302

The Ragtime Dream, performed by the American Quartet 1914
http://www.loc.gov/jukebox/recordings/detail/id/3630

Yiddisha Nightingale (1911)
http://www.loc.gov/jukebox/recordings/detail/id/2404

Dill Pickles Rag by Chris Chapman (1908)
Xylophone
http://www.loc.gov/jukebox/recordings/detail/id/1416

Alexander's Ragtime Band (1911)
http://www.loc.gov/jukebox/recordings/detail/id/2259

Ragtime Violin by Irving Berlin
http://www.loc.gov/jukebox/recordings/detail/id/2514 (Dec. 15, 1911)

El Mole Rachmin

The Irish, The Irish

Be British
http://www.nmni.com/titanic/Home/Audio-(1)/Be-Belfast.aspx

Postcard advertising the song
The lost Titanic.
For voice.
First line: She was the biggest ship afloat.
Refrain: I'm sinking, sinking, sinking far out on the
ocean.

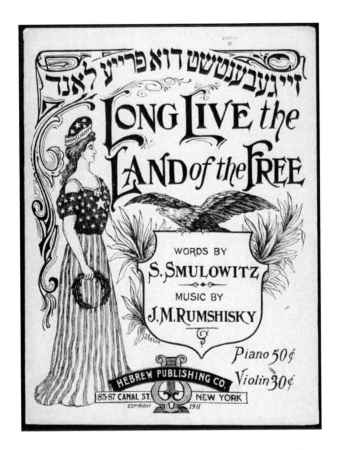

"Land of the Free," a comic song but unabashedly patriotic, delivers impassioned lyrics that describe the hope and fierce loyalty many immigrants felt for America.

The lyrics read:

"Every Jew must express his loyalty to the Land of Freedom with all his being/Once settled he will surely appreciate a Land which gives him full and equal rights/

Yes! Yes!/ So become a citizen, take out the required papers/
Oy, Oy/ Become an in-law of Uncle Sam/ Cast your vote/ It gives you great power/ Then none can cause you hurt/ The world will esteem the Jew/ Defend the American Flag."

A body being fished from the sea by a recovery crew from Halifax.

Section Three

THE WRECK OF THE TITANIC

By Horace Greeley

***DEDICATED TO HER EIGHT MUSICIANS:*HARTLEY, HUME, TAYLOR, CLARK, WOODWARD, BRAILEY, KRINS, AND BREICOUX**

WHEN THOUGHTS TURN TO THE HEREAFTER.

By John T. McCutcheon.

"**We** dedicate this verse to you who died,
Undaunted bandsmen eight, where side by side
You braved the demon Fear so few indeed
Could feel the pangs on which he's wont to feed;
Tight drew your courage with your violin string,
And every note sprung vibrant with its ring,
So music's endless chain in your control
Held up men's hearts and tempered every soul;
Enforced with yours their valor stood the test,
And showed when we must die how 'tis done best.
Whence came your spirit? Needs more than your race
'Mid whom your forebear minstrels marked the pace
To which its heroes wrought their deeds sublime.
Kindling a flame to glorify their time.
In many stories that we've read of old,
Of daring exploits, sacrifices bold,
None have surpassed this deed superbly done,
None greater glory than yourselves have won.
So shall we crown you with those laurel wreaths
Which as his due each noblest man receives.
And on each bay we'll write in measured line
The true, sad story ye have made divine!

The love of travel and its changing view,
Whichever brings to one impressions new,
Rejuvenates the mind as much as sleep.
For, when our senses have been furrowed deep
By one impress, adjoining substance may
Receive another in another way;
And after this awhile has entertained

The wearied takes its place with strength regained.
While some enjoy such pleasures as they list.
To most they come but with that golden mist
That rises from our thoughts when dreaming o'er
The script of pilgrims from some other shore:
Among these most a few there always are
Who formulate this haze into a star
Which leads them vainly on to find, it seems,
What they should hope for only in their dreams;
Still home and friends, their scanty hoard are cast
Where soon the enchantment of the future gilds
the past.

Of such the burden the *Titanic* bore:
The idler, whom we oft should credit more —
For leisure breeds the thoughts that lead the wise,
Without it how could man philosophize?
The emigrant, much nearer to the soil,
Whose hope to rise from bread-and-butter toil
Lies in the fate the future holds away
That chance will favor him in some strange way;
And then the merchant, counting o'er his store.
How by new scheming he may make it more,
Regretting pleasure oft, if nothing gained —
The frugal habit's strict when once obtained;
"Industry's Cavalier" on forage bent.
Good losing lambs, it seems, are always sent;
There were the lovers, seeking many skies
To view their beauties in each other's eyes;
And then those great men, who, when seen afar.
Cause wonder as the fabled child felt for the star.

Four days at sea on such a pleasure boat

Brought no sea-knowledge but they were afloat;
For so elaborate had the builder's art
Outfitted her that all might from the start
Imagine they stopped at some beach hotel
That fashion sought in lazy comfort dwell;
The decks on which they sat or idly strolled
Piazzas looking seaward where they lolled.
And so upon the fourth, a Sunday's eve,
No thought of danger could a soul conceive;
A concert some attended, some a prayer.
Some played at cards, few tempted the chill air;
While others visited their new made friends,
Discussed at length their journey and its ends;
At dinner-parties, some made merry late,
Where jovial friends together drank and ate;
Till growing quietude closed o'er the day
And drove the most to bed fatigue would not obey.

The sea is calm, the night is cold and clear,
No rocks are nigh, what should a staunch ship fear?
The bridge is paced, the crow's-nest watch is manned,
The saving wireless ready to command —
What was the message that the Captain told
From other ships o'er ether's waves had rolled?
That in advance of their wave cleaving prow
A fleet of icebergs hovered, hover now!
Such news the watch had often heard before,
Its warnings hazard always said ignore;
So forward by the glowing starry light
Sped on the ship with naught to fear in sight.

What was it Murdock thought of on the bridge.

As to-and-fro on that commanding ridge
He paced? What else but his dear English home,
Which, though his calling dragged him forth to
roam.
Held all his love, ambition and his care.
And drew on sigh-wing's wafture his true spirit there!

A bashful man, he long admired aside,
Restrained by her deserving and his pride;
Both these so balanced that it seemed in vain
To hope the one the other might overstrain
So he could speak the craving prayer he felt
And stand where now devotion mutely knelt ;
His latest furlough o'er he sought her last
To bid adieu, he thought, as in the past ;
But as he faltered out a last farewell,
As many merging ripples raise a swell,
All the restrained emotions of the past
Surged to his brain and had their way at last.

So oft it is the case that women know
What lies ahead and when a wind shall blow
'Tis long expected, so her ready sail
Caught in the breeze and let the breeze prevail.
She made the home-land, England, doubly dear,
Through husband-lover's eyes a paradise appear!
How can we hope when we so truly know

That all we rear can ne'er escape the blow
That nature has in store for each apart,
For all that build a mind or mould a heart;
That as we struggle to a higher state
The pangs grow keener, harder still our fate!

Murdock, be firm, for now the chancing's near
That visits all, both those who brave or fear!
Three bells are heard, the lookout 'phones in haste,
And hard-a-starboard is the rudder placed;
But all too late, for though she swerves away
The power that sped her on must have its play,
And on a darkly cowering iceberg arrives
The greatest ship that ever bore human lives!

The engines quickly stopped, the bulkheads closed.
The crew all called to stations — those who dozed
Were barely wakened by the gentle jar,
Much like a row-boat scraping o'er a rocky bar!
Lieutenant Murdock turns, the Captain greets,
In hurried words the happening repeats;
Quick orders issued bid them sound the hold,
But news already comes, ill's quickly told,
That water's rising everywhere below
So fast that pumps were useless, that the blow
Cut through the steel clad monster's under-side
As sword-fish pierces whale in battle glide!

The skipper bit his lip and gripped the rail,
But quickly rallying said, "None of you fail
To assure those whom we now must quickly wake
We launch the boats but for precaution's sake;
She cannot sink, else panic may prevail
And spread disorder over all avail;
Take women first and children, all ye may;
Take out all boats and quickly pull away,
Within an hour we'll rest beneath the wave.

But courage holding, mates, there're some we'll
surely save!"
He bids the wireless boys to thrill the air
And call responding ships to their despair;

Then soon there comes an answering quiver back
Three trembling ships bear hard upon their track,
Their captains turn them from their destined
course
And forward to the rescue, at full force!
A boat unlimbered dangles o'er the rail,
But hardly with a few can they prevail
To leave the ship, which yet but slightly lists,
Such needless care their confidence resists;
On decks so solid need the timid quail?
To trust the ocean in a thing so frail
Would surely be the quickest way to drown!
Still o'er the side some nineteen rattle down,

And seventy feet below rest on the sea
So tranquil that 'twas strange that such could be,
For gurgles, ripples to every move respond
As on the placid surface of a garden pond!
Two sailors and a 'master made the crew,
And fast away the tiny vessel drew;
They pulled ahead to make a guiding light
Borne on a ship some distance off, in sight.
"Be that your haven," said the Captain last,
"Unload your boat and here again make fast."

Meanwhile the steamer's Morse light-signals flash,
Appealing rockets skyward make their dash,
And bombs resound to draw attention where

70

Quick aid is needed, else the most despair!
For deep her bow is settling in the tide
As other boats swing loaded o'er the side;
As one descends, beneath is heard a roar,
And then is seen a threatening torrent pour —
*Tis what the pumps throw out, though but in vain.
Too great the gash they struggle against to gain!
A whirlwind could not draw that water out
In its most mighty, thirsty, draining water-spout!

With ropes still clinging, drifting on the sea,
Now none can find the pin to set them free.
And o'er their heads descends another boat;
This stopped in time by warning from each throat
Beneath its keel, gives chance a moment's play,
And out they swing with tackle cut away!
The deluge whirls them 'round in time to face
The other boat just landed in their place.
Upon the ship assurance now subsides.
And in its place restrained emotion hides.
For fast the tilt increases, decks descend,
And none may now but reason of the end.
Upon the port side Murdock clears away,
Lightoller on the starboard all obey,
While from the bridge the Captain views the light
Approach and veer, soon fading out of sight.

What were his thoughts no one may ever tell,
But for the most all hope passed on, this he knew
well!
"Accursed Captain of yon passing boat,
Flow can you live, how can you keep afloat?
These signals in plain view your sense must feel,

71

And yet away you turn your dogged keel!
What though the ice be nigh, or danger great,
How can you pass and leave us to our fate?
If but a spark of what we call a soul
Could in your carcass live would all control.
Veer round your helm; your engines drive full
speed.

In glorious rapture spring to meet our need!
But no, if ever such in your foul heart
Implanted at your birth its growth could start
'Twas early smothered by your muddy blood.
And nurtured by this filthy sluggish flood
Your mind became the thing that turns away
When drowning brothers cry for aid to-day!
Though all would live still here is none so low
Who'd 'change his dying state with yours, full well I
know !"

If thus it was the Captain felt and thought
To wordy utterance 'twas never brought.
Perhaps he knew that such a common thing,
Neglect of others, small reproach might bring;
Familiar, doubtless, was to averted look.
The hastened step that misery forsook;
"I have no time, let others lend their aid,"
With which the nearest ones such tasks evade;
Or else he left both judgment and repay
Where he believed effective power lay!
Whichever it was let us who hear the tale
Survivors brought in harrowing detail.

Be not too rash; in haste lay not our curse
On stupid carelessness, perhaps, for worse;

But as the signaled ship passed by unnamed,
Let us pass by her skipper still un-blamed;
Yet were he guilty, punishment there's none
Could reach the quick less sense of such a
hardened one!

The later life-boats tense their tackle strain,
For most are eager seats therein to gain;
Full seventy souls were safe within, afloat,
But in the launching, such a heavy boat
Might spring a seam or even rift a rope;
So caution by a third reduced their scope.
Fifteen young bridegrooms thrust unwilling brides,
Speechless from anguish, sobbing, from their sides,
But cheerily still in word, if not in heart;
"Goodbye, my love, but for a time we part,
Your safety first assured, I'll follow fast.
Goodbye, one kiss, until the next 'twill last."
"My Lucien, can't my Lucien come with me?
There's room enough, hold sir. Oh heed my plea!"

But quick the order, quicker spin the wheels,
The boat descends, the sweet-faced girl-wife reels.
And, caught by calmer sufferers by her side.
Now lives, the tender nobleness of him who died!
But some refuse, more sober age has brought
Keener perception, better gauging thought;
Whatever chance there is, they will not take,
That he may follow, naught but force can make
Them leave the side by which so long they've stood
Averting evil, welcoming the good;
So these draw back, the worse prefer to bear,
Disdaining better if he cannot share.

"Sometime we've been together, come what may
Now or henceforth, together we shall stay;

In youth I took thine arm, I grasp it now
To follow thy good fortune, or to bow
To all Jehovah sends of what is ill,
With the same spirit and the same good will;
Without thee all were desolate and dead.
All good were evil, evil in its stead.
With thee to lean upon, seems naught to fear;
'Tis likewise with thyself towards me, so I stay
here!"
Thus spoke, O Israel! All thy daughters' worth,

Great as this has been since thy race's birth.
Incarnate in one soul that fear defied!
This woman's glory, let it be thy pride,
And, as a token ye remember well,
When each shall journey o'er the ocean's swell.
And passing off the ridge that marks the banks
Newfoundland claims and the Atlantic flanks,
Let each one drop a stone upon that wave
Where she once stood and which now marks her
grave.

That all these stones together soon may rise
Three thousand fathoms up to meet the skies!
Though millions into millions must be rolled
To make this sum, let resolution hold;
For none deny the tribute due today,
Nor will the future its respects delay —
All love to aid to liquidate a debt

Incurred for such a lesson, such example set!

Upon the topmost deck all boats were stowed,
And here a few took in a partial load,
To then be lowered to the rail below
Where, orders were, the women all must go.
Here many men the present world knew well
Stood back and calmly waved their last farewell;
For education, worldly wisdom's gain
Had taught each one the pride which scorns all
pain,
That he who yields to terror for his life
Saves what is hardly worth such lowly strife;

For never after may his spirit swell
With inner pride which each of us loves well —
This wastes away without its mother's mead,
"Few or none other would have done my deed,"
And lacking this we crawl away our time,
Hiding beneath stones as worms enrapt in slime,
While he who dies unmoved, though well aware.
Mounts in this pride beyond all other men's
compare!
One of these men a little boy befriends,
Who'd been turned back, and his distress soon
ends;
For, clapping on his head a feathered hat,
"My lad, a woman now you are with that!"
And him, with many others, hands along
Into the boats from out the waiting throng.
They say that here a soldier proved his right
In modern times to spurs of ancient knight;

Ah! Major Butt, who envies not the name
You leave emblazoned on the role of fame!
May all of us partake that last farewell
You waved to one who knew and loved you well,
"Remember me to all the folks back home.
Goodbye, good luck be with you as you roam!"
And let us love and cherish with this man
All those whose valor made them of his clan —
The many heroes at whose names Report,
    Subject to tyrant Chance, perhaps has never
caught!

One brave, unselfish girl gave up her place
In a last boat, remained behind to face,
That no strange sister might step out for her,
All danger's threatening, for the orders were
That one too many packed the fragile shell.
Which like a leaf hurled trembling o'er the swell;
Then, though the cry resounded, "Lower away!"
The strong arms at the ropes a moment stay
As two babes in a blanket in are thrust,
Where willing arms receive the orphaned trust;
Down shoots the boat, but from a deck below
Out springs a man, whose rushing body's blow
Strikes from her seat a woman o'er the side,
At whom some grasp, but sinks into the tide;
Within another, steadied at the rail.
Two just have stepped when, frenzied past avail

By rising waters which put them to rout,
    A swarming crew of stokers seize and swing her
out!
The boats are gone, half loaded it may be,

But who's the fault? In fear away they flee,
Forgetting those now left behind to drown,
Lest the now trembling wreck engulf them down —

All thought that's left to this they now devote.
None heed the order given, "When afloat.
All boats around the gang-way ladder bring,
There on your oars till further orders swing!"
Now all those left aboard realize their case;
How many took it let it be our place,
As far as we are guided by those tales
That reason may allow of what avails,
To here record as clearly as we can;
Remembering always that we deal with man.

Not a Minerva from a god-head burst,
Nor one created perfect at the first.
But one who's ever moulded of the dust,
From which derive his actions, be they wrong or
just!
When first the Captain knew the damage done
He ordered life-belts placed on every one,
And on the topmost deck, with gayest air,

The band to buoy all hearts against despair.
In music's strains depicted others woe,
By all the happy, may unheeded flow;
But when the real is felt in all its might.
With all its venomed barbs in wildest flight.
The staunchest hearts to lightest notes will spring
To catch the tempo and so dull its sting!

And now, though many ragtime airs were played.

Still rallying were they to the heart dismayed;
Yet most of all was the example set
By those eight bandsmen, whom we'll ne'er forget!
While yet the tilting deck a foothold gave.
Rang out their dirge triumphant of the brave!
None more! for where should courage' acme lie
If not where death is calmly viewed approaching
nigh!
Of course, in logic we may reason much
Of how so many escaped wild panic's clutch;
For very few, indeed, gave way to fear,

Even when all knew catastrophe was near:
No crash was felt, to such a mighty blow
The inch steel plates gave way, as banks of snow
Before a plow's steel-clad oncoming beak.
And crumpled inward from the icy peak;
The air was calm, the ocean quiet lay,
The ship lay steadied in a normal way;
No gash was seen, and the increasing list,
The throbbing tremor of the engines missed.
The hiss of steam blown off, the rocket's glare.
Were all that told something had happened there;
The life-preservers and the boats were deemed
Precautions greater than the danger seemed;
Attentive apprehension held them all.
But no rude violence shocked and no strange scene
appalled!

'Tis thus when illness thralls us we behave,
Even though 'tis dragging to a certain grave,
And none cry out unless distress and pain.
By sudden onset, mastery obtain;

Though what we dread most hangs but by a hair,
Yet all still feel that time and chance may spare;
Mere fear of what's been never felt before
Seems in the future dim as ancient lore;
Still the suspense upon the settling deck
Drives some to seek diversion's certain check,
Which, as a safety valve, lets out the press
Of sworn emotions when they most distress;
Within the smokers' cabin cards are seen.
The stakes much greater than before had been;
They shuffle, deal, and play with nervous speed.
And for their game alone, it seems, have heed;
No counters o'er the broadcloth's verdure roll.
Each here may win the prize, the prize of self-
control!

The smoker's comfort steadies many friends.
And wine, that worry poison, also lends
Its force to those whose sluggish hearts require
Its power to drive, whose brains its added fire.
At exercises in the gymnasts' hall
Some raise the bells, and other roll the ball,
Pull at false oars, or ride the camel's back
O'er an imagined desert's sandy track;
Some stalwart souls supremely stoic stand.
Or hold a friend or brother by the hand;
In little groups are gathered, huddled near.
Some fathers, mothers, and their children dear—
For from the cabins some have missed the boats,
And of the steerage, a survivor notes.
But those the second cabin's fleet could share
Were of the lucky chancing choose to spare;
Spared but for other days, as woe but waits.

At every door, the juggling of the wanton Fates!

But scorn all comfort! Help is past avail!
Deceit, though seeming pleasant's for the frail!
No balm's in Gilead that can cause to bear
The stifling process, death, unmoved, aware!
Call not for medicine, no physician's there.
But resolution which may make all dare!
'Tis sickening to the brave to half conceal
Amid unfelt phantasms what is real!
Far better 'tis to face the bitter truth,
Well knowing when for us there is no ruth!
This Murdock knows, and feels its heavy hand
That bears on him, on him who held command
When the great ship ripped off her bosom's shield,
And sixteen hundred's fate an instant sealed!
Until all boats were launched he hardly knew
The moments passed, so quickly 'round he flew;
A boat swung out and loaded, lowered away.
One after one his care saw safely under way!

And now the last boat in the tackle lies,
Stuck 'mid the davits whose defect denies
His every effort made to swing her free
O'er bulwarks fast descending to the sea!
Whatever he could is done, this moment now
He owes himself, the last the Fates allow!
Small choice is his, to stiffen 'mid the ice,
Or die the master, neither may entice!
And yet 'tis comforting to know we hold
A power so absolute, when we are bold!
For bolder 'tis to face inflicted death.
When 'tis ourselves who speed the parting breath,

Than when it wins against the feeble strife
We may oppose, when most we crave for life!

Let him who 'Coward' cries, crawl to his end,
Bearing affliction that he dares not mend;
For still the more we live the greater grows
The dearth of pleasures and the sum of all our
woes!
Murdock knew this, and yet he dared to find
A constant pleasure to please one ever kind;
'Twas this he found the only holding tie
That interfered with his content to die —
Reciprocating love drives on two souls
Through much that's bitter, for each ever holds
Fast to that purpose which most pleases both—
Affection binds those who'd neglect an oath —

To save the other from the world's annoy.
To add what might be to his dream of joy!
But Oh! 'tis ever, as 'twas now the trend
Of all contentment, woe lies at the end!
Thus is it wise to entwine two fragile lives
So close that loss of one at once deprives
The other of that power to hope which gives
Inciting motive, without which who lives?
For her his heartache multiplied the pain
He felt for others sorrows, both now all in vain!
The ship now trembles in her final throe!
He must prepare, for with her he must go!
Were his such a chance, escape he must deny,
He drove her on, and with her he must die!
One choice is his, he may anticipate.
Or, like one held for slaughter, dumbly wait!

A brain awhirl, for action ever makes,
His case seems clear, so quick again he takes
That potent weapon which before he drew
To hold in check the maddened stoker crew;
Crack! goes the shell remaining, crack the shell
Where in such thoughts impetuous might not
dwell!
Murdock, adieu, much honor on thy name.
May all thy fellows share immortal fame!
Self-speed as thou, some say, were others too,
Their duty done, death all that lay in view —
Among immortals it might be a prize
More great than life eternal to our glazing eyes!

The wireless lads still splutter at their task,
Locate their ship and speedy rescue ask
Of all they reach, tell how the water gains;
But soon their efforts cease, the current wanes,
Stops short their signal, waves lap at their door,
The Captain shouts to tarry there no more!
But Phillips tries again, to danger blind,
And, as he works, a stoker creeps behind,
Unfasts his lifebelt, to his aid young Bride
Springs with a wrench, the thief floors at his side!
They quit their cabin, Phillips hastens aft,
While Bride joins some now tugging at a raft

Bestowed above the chartroom, which they throw
Upon the boat-deck now awash below;
The bow swings downward, all are washed afloat,

Most of its launchers clinging to the boat;

An instant later, falling on their track,
A monster funnel fell and threw her on her back!

Up to the bridge the bow is covered over,
Fast sinking in the water, more and more,
The ship must soon pass far below the wave;
This knows the Captain, one more yet he'll save!
So grasping tight an infant found astray.
Into the sea he plunges, swims away
Unto the nearest lifeboat standing by,
And hands within his charge to those who try
To next reach for him, but he waves them back.
Disdaining rescue he knows others lack!

"Where's Murdock? Cannot one within there tell?"
"He shot himself, I saw him when he fell!"
To this brave Captain Smith gives no reply,
Strips off his lifebelt, vents a single sigh,
And, facing for a moment toward his ship
Whose stern swings high, both in the ocean slip!
Good bye, good Captain, well you learnt in life
To meet the worst that comes to man in peace or
strife!

While this was taking place Lightoller stood
Upon the Captain's quarters, near the hood
The fore lee blower swung to catch the air;
A moment pausing, hesitating there,
He feels the vessel's bow drop in the deep;
So, springing outward in a desperate leap,
He strives to clear the engulfing wave's rebound,
But 'tis in vain, the suction drags him 'round;

Beneath the sea, again the blower 's near.
An airy gust ascending lifts him clear;
Once more submerged, the fiddley-grating feels;
But, ere his brain to suffocation yields,
Again a gaseous force blows him to light,
The stars before his eyes now set in night!
He sees the capsized boat, on it he crawls,
And views a scene his hardy heart appalls,

As others seek asylum on the raft.
Till thirty tightly pack the unsteady, tiny craft!
The ship had settled while her list to port
But slowly grew, and lapping waters sought
The upper deck, along her sloping side,
As gently rising o'er some shore, the tide;
Her bow first under, glowing port-holes shone
In lines aslant to meet the liquid zone.
One after one cut off, as lower yet
They passed beneath where air and water met.
At last, when ripples reached the chartroom door.
And while abaft the deck was covered over
With surging crowds, no longer held in check.
Each class apart on its appropriate deck;
While still our bandsmen played, undaunted, there,
And notes of "Autumn" thrilled the chilly air;
The prow swung downward, high the rudder
reared,
The lights went out, the end to all appeared ;
For from the trembling wreck was heard a roar,
As loosened engines, crashing, through her entrails
tore!

The engineers! Who gives them even a thought?

So often 'tis when simple duty's wrought
Where none may see, none clarion forth in praise,
Nor note the merit in the after days.
No wonder, then, some hope for just reward
From abstract justice, which they name the Lord!
Our hope obscures, our pride denies, our fate.
While Cosmos yawns and cleans again her slate!
The thirty engineers, and more, remained
Below to labor, every chance disdained!
For here they knew escape might never hap,
And vain their efforts against the lengthy gap!
They drove the pumps, and drew each fire when
neared
The rising water; till the last they cheered
All those above with that great solace, light;
Kept till the end the ship illumined bright!
Then with their engines crashing to their grave!
Could ever men more merit, could they be more
brave?

Almost upright the keel a moment stands,
While some still cling to railings with their hands,
And sparks from out an after funnel leap;
But for a moment though, for dipping deep,
Almost as softly as the stricken duck
That diving cheats the sportsman of his luck,
The great Titanic sinks to vales below.
Where o'er her grave two miles of ocean flow!
One sprang from off the poop, just as she sped.
Saw her enormous screws just miss his head;
And, swimming to the bottom-upturned boat,

Crawled on, the last who thus was kept afloat.

How died the sixteen hundred left behind.
Each in a futile life preserver 'twined?
Let tell the tale a bride who fondly thought
In later boats than hers all would be brought;
Let her repeat the record scored by pain;
A record, let us hope, will ne'er be writ again!

"I sat benumbed beside an idle oar,
Within a boat 'round which were gathered more,
Benumbed by thought that all so strange excites
Until its raging, through fatigue, requites;
I saw the ship, in silence, settle fast;
No voice, no sound; I saw her sink at last!
'My love, with others, now is safe afloat,
'Somewhere around, within another boat,'

I heard one say, and so we all believed;
But for a moment, though, were so deceived;
For o'er the water from the mile away
A cry resounded unto where we lay;
A cry, Oh God! Must I describe the sound.
The yelps of dogs, in frightful medley wound!
It rose, it fell, in gasps then came again,
The dying protest of those freezing men!
The horror of that moment thrills me yet,
And none who heard that cry, while living can
forget!

To think, but ah, what now avails the thought!
A few more boats, such life were cheaply bought!
Those who survived, as I, were spared the pain,
That numbing ache from which escape is vain!
Of life prolonged beyond ambition's death.

Whose drag's increased by each succeeding breath.
Yet time even this will cure, a hundred years
Will carry all beyond their utmost fears;
One then as all will be, true friends or foes.
Where pleasures lead so also will our woes!
This is so near, the weary should take heart,
None, none should fear the ending as the start!
Yet Oh! why reason thus, while still I crave
That dear companion whom I could not save!
Thou demon. Cannot, sere no more my brain!
Forgetfulness, haste thou to ease my pain!
But no, what use is logic 'against the will.
For dear Remembrance is my constant idol still!"

Upon the capsized boat the thirty crowd,
So tightly packed no room to move is allowed —
The wireless boys are here, and also two
Who had been passengers, the rest were crew —
While gasping men swim up and turn away,
Their feeble question hoarsely answered, nay;
Such visits cease, the icy water's chill
Soon stiffens muscles and benumbs the will.
And then around but nodding corpses float,
Who've lost the cares of those upon the boat!
These, all awash and soaked with frigid brine,
Arrange themselves along the keel in line;
And back to back, with water to their knees,
Await a rescue or their turn to freeze!
But some too weak to stand lie half afloat.
Jack Phillips one, one in a soldier's coat,
Who soon relax and slip into the sea;
Exhaustion overcoming frail mortality!

Some lifeboats, clustered near a mile away,
About a lantern lashed together lay;
None ventured back, although all heard the cry —
The cry that called for aid on all nearby!
Some were too full, and some had none to row;
At least 'tis argued thus they could not go;
They managed, still, to reach their mooring place,
And, later, even to move off a space.
Of women some held all but three or four;
One boat a man in woman's clothing bore;
In one eight Chinamen themselves bestowed;
And few among them all had ever rowed.
'Tis certain many seemed completely dazed,
And some, perhaps, the moment even crazed;
For, as one boat moved from its launching place,
A woman struck a swimmer on the face;
And, when the others hauled him in the boat,
His cheek was bloody where her diamonded hand
had smote!

A human heart at last asserts its sway!
The selfish brain, abashed, in one gives way!
And Lowe transfers to boats but partly filled,
Against protests effected as he willed.
His load of souls, unfurls his little sail,
And makes for whence no longer comes a wail;
But three he finds afloat and yet alive,
So few an hour, it seems, could thus survive;
And one of these, is it not strange to note,
Is very drunk when drawn aboard the boat;
Perhaps he thought would make a faint heart bold.
Or warm him against the water's icy cold!
Now back again the lifeboat's helm is set.

Without sufficient search, else had it met
The silent thirty floating on the keel.
Now so benumbed that they have ceased to feel!

Yet back in time to opportunely save
A leaking lifeboat's load fast sinking in the wave!
Now must all wait, no power but this is theirs:
The land's beyond their reach, starvation stares
A few days off at most, and should the sea
Arise in fury, helpless all would be!
But still they comfort, all had heard before
That several ships hard on their reckonings bore;
Perhaps ere daylight one may reach the place,
So through the glimmer peers each eager face.
What is that light which glitters now afar!
Is it a vessel? No, another star;
Another one of those afar-off-things
That thoughts of other than the present brings

In streaming light, which by our blinking eyes
From dimmest past to distant future flies;
May one imagine how it had its birth,
Or where its flashes end that pass our earth?
A link within the circle of Always
Which none may measure, counted in our tale of
days!
Horizon to the zenith shone this night,
So clear the air, with every starry light;
Even where the arching sky the water met,
Some twinkled over the edge, while others set,
Abruptly dipping on the western side
As though their pathway led below the tide.
And oft deceived by these were those who sought

To be the first to spy the succor brought;
Yet on they watch; at last a glow is seen.
Perhaps the moon, is that her silvery sheen?
Now just above the water peeps the light.
And its reflection breaks upon their sight
In glancing rays along the sleeping sea;
If not the moon, perhaps. Oh, it must be —
Oh, yes it is, for see the rocket rise,
In wavering lines ascend into the skies —
They hear its boom soon follow from afar —
Suspended breaths escaping all in chorused "AH!"

Some minutes short of midnight came the blow,
At two-and-twenty she had sunk below;
And now two hours later comes that aid
The wireless summoned that Marconi made —
Great credit be to him, and unto all
Who helped develop the electric call
That sped to Captain Rostron on his way
Some sixty miles of ocean off, they say;
And unto him, this captain, brave and true, "
What credit could repay one-half his due!
Who drove his ship by 'bergs, through fields of ice.
Far off her course, alone for honor's price!
Yet pause to think, he best loves honor's mead
Who most is worthy, does the noblest deed;
And this, which needs no eulogistic phrase
To place with those far past the reach of praise,
Exalts this man to ever rank with those
AH class, revere, or even worship as heroes!

Meanwhile the ship, her searchlight glowing bright,
Approaches nearer to an out-hung light

One boat displays, with slow and cautious tread;
But ere 'tis reached an iceberg stops her dead.
Maneuvering 'round, the sea is free between.
Where she awaits the swaying light of green;
Alongside soon, while spreads the morning's glow.
The rescued scale a ladder from below;

While at the rail the Captain and his crew,
And of the steamer's passengers a few.
Extend the care and welcome they require;
Help all within, unto their least desire.
The dawning now discloses 'round the place
A troop of icebergs, over the water's face
The sixteen boats approaching from between:
The stars are fading, but the moon is seen
Just rising o'er a peak of glowing ice —
The scene indeed was thrilling. Oh, at such a price!

One of the lifeboats met, just ere the dawn,
Those floating on the raft so cold and worn
That two died after transfer, three were sent
Aboard the saving liner so far spent
The little life flame left them flickered out
Before, almost, her bow was put about;
Although the others, saving very few
Who'd been frostbitten, had a bruise or two,
Of all the five and seven hundred saved.
Were very well and normally behaved;

Even those who'd lost a loved one in the wreck
Could but feel thankful on a solid deck;
And most of these still hoped for many a day
He had been saved in some yet unknown way.

With all aboard, the steamer cruised around
In hope that others living might be found;
Some tables, chairs, a hatchway grate, afloat,
Was all, 'tis said, they saw, besides the overturned
boat.

And yet some hours later there were found,
Still floating upright, life-preserver bound.
Four hundred corpses over the same area,
By those expressly sent to seek them here.
As if to saddest things to further add,
For past extremity there's naught more sad.
These also caught beneath a crested wave,
That rocked it gently in its cradled grave,

A naked babe, lost from the mother's breast.
Who doubtless till the last had closely pressed.
And, ere it fell from out her helpless arms.
Had deeply drunk of euthanasia's balms;
Who was she, none could tell, a thousand more,
With her, the ship into the ocean bore;
Some clung to railings, some, 'tis but surmise.
Were waked by rushing waters, in surprise,
Or else were suffocated in their sleep
When she plunged headlong far beneath the
overwhelming deep!

And further on, a father with his arm
Around his boy, a shield from threatening harm;
Though chilled to death both yet retained their
grasp,
Locked firmer still with each expiring gasp!
And there, a mother holding o'er her head,

Above the freezing waters both had sped,
The cherished child she had not power to save.
Though all her strength upheld it from the wave!
How did she comfort it, what did she say.
Before exhaustion stole her speech away?
What could she promise then, how ease its fright.
Alone, 'mid chilling waters, in the night?
Oh, what can you, or I, or anyone

Bespeak their offspring ere the future 's run!
A fate unknown, a little breathing space,
But the same end though varied be the race!
The choice is small, although we know it not.
Because all live to die, and dying have forgot!
Renewed 's the journey, from the icy peaks
Along a lengthy floe Carpathia seeks
The open sea — Ah, had they known this strand
Was floating near, so easy 'twas to land.
Another story might have been to tell —
And, after three days more upon the swell,
Lands the forlorn, though grateful, folk at last.
Where we shall leave them, sheltered in the vast

Outpourings of a sympathetic world —
Not that with mourning banner wide unfurled.
More for its selfish self than the bereaved —
But it whose tear apart, and want relieved
Help all to feel there is a home yet left
Where there's even solace for the most bereft—
For that poor child who searched the steamer
through,
"I do not see them," and the widowed too —
By this's not meant to what befell that day

One could be reconciled, or aught such loss repay!
Among those scenes intense emotion swayed
Upon the landing pier two may not fade;
They show so well the careless hand of Fate
That strikes on this too soon, on that too late:
The pale young girl who waited through the night,
Beside the empty gangway till daylight;
Whom she expected, none could make her say.
But shook her head and watched the vacant way;
She spoke to none, and none dared press her
more.

None saw her leave for all left long before;
Within her breast such silent sorrow slept
She doubtless feared to lose as those who wept.
Alone she came, alone she stood apart;
Alone she left in loneliness of heart!
Hers never came, another stepped ashore, ^
A bent old man whose gaze was fixed before;
None came for him, he looked to neither side.
And straightway fled the scene with hastened
lengthy stride!

Since early time we've wished to turn all blame,
And so a scapegoat takes at least the name;
Thus here, some say, the Captain went too fast,
Or that the builders built her far too vast;
Reproach the line for placing boats so few
That all could never enter them, it knew;
Forgetting, first, demand, and then, the law
That specified but what the vessel bore.
Forbear to censure, fear 'twill hap again,
Blame no one singly for the fault of men;
Nor weep today for what is past redress.

For twill but add a new to old distress.
Let those who lost their loved ones know again
The best that haps to all postpones their pain;
That those who've gone may never feel it more,
But we who linger have it ever in store;
However we play, at last we lose, the same.
And when most lucky may but chose the final
game!

WALLACE H. HARTLEY.

NATIVE OF COLNE.

The "Titanic's" Heroic Musical Conductor.

WHO LOST HIS LIFE IN THE DISASTER.

APRIL 15th. 1912.

Mail being loaded on the Titanic at Queenstown, Ireland. Below, Capt. E. J. Smith.

This poem was written by Father Frank Browne (who left Titanic when she docked in Ireland)

"IN MEMORIAM"

"April 15th,1912"

"A ship rode forth on the Noonday tide
 Rode forth to the open sea
 and high sun shone on the good ship's side,
 And all seemed gladness, and hope, and pride
 For the gallant sight she was"

"For the crew was strong, and the captain brave
 And never a fear had they,
 Never a thought for the turbulent wave,
 Never a dread of a watery grave,
 Nor dreams of a fateful day."

"So the ship sailed on, and the voices strong
 Sang sweet on the morning air,
 And the glad notes billowed the shore along,
 they drifted and died, till the Sailors' song
 Was soft as a whispered prayer"

"And all seemed gladness, and hope ,and pride
 As far as the eye could see,
 For where was the foe that could pierce her side,
 Or where in the Ocean depths could hide,
 A mightier power then she?"

"But far to the North, in the frozen zone

Where the Ice King holds his sway,
Full many a berg, like the monarch's throne
Or castle that fabled princes own
Gleamed white neath the Sun's bright ray"

"When the challenge came on the whisp'ring air
It passed like a fleeting breath,
But it roused a king in his Arctic lair,
And waked what vengeance was sleeping there,
The vengeance of Doom and Death"

"But heedless and gay o'er the sunlit waves
The vessel all lightly bore,
Till the distant coast with its rocks and caves,
And the land that the Western Ocean laves,
Were seen from her decks no more"

"When Evening came with the waning light,
And shrouded the rolling deep,
For never a moment she stayed her flight,
Adown the path of the moonbeams bright,
Though Heaven was wrapped in sleep."

"Another dawn with its liquid gold
Gilded the Eastern sky
Lighting the ship so fair, so bold
that sped its way o'er the Ocean old,
Nor wrecked of danger nigh...."

"And noonday came, when the burning sun
Rifted the realms of snow
And burst the fetters the Ice had spun

And shattered the towers that Cold had won,
Breaking the great Ice-flow"

"Till over the ocean's heaving swells,
Like ghosts in the twilight gloom,
The great bergs glided with purpose fell
Minding the quest of their Monarch well,
The quest of Revenge and Doom"

" The deeper night with it slow advance
Bids even the winds to cease,
No moonbeams bright on the waters dance
But all lie still in a starry trance
And the Ocean sleeps in peace"

"A shuddering gasp o'er the resting deep!
A wail from the silent sea!
Tis heard where the stars their lone watch keep
Tis heard in the grave where the dead men sleep,
mindful of human glee...

"The Springtime dawn with its rosy light
See naught but the waves' wild flow
For under the veil of the moonless night
When the sea was still and the stars were bright
The Ice King had slain his foe."

"The Ship that rode on noonday tide
Rode forth to open sea,
But gone are the gladness, and hope, and pride
For the Northern Ocean's depths could hide
A mightier power than she."

THE SCENE OUTSIDE THE WHITE STAR OFFICES AT SOUTHAMPTON

SIX STOWAWAY CHINESE ESCAPE

Disguised as Women, They Secure Places in Lifeboat.
(Special to The Richmond Times-Dispatch)

New York. April, 20, 1912 Among those rescued from the sinking Titanic were six Chinese, who had stowed themselves away in one of the vessel's lifeboats before she left England. When the crash came on Sunday night the Chinese did not become excited. They knew the lifeboat would be lowered if there was any danger of the giant Titanic going down. All had shawls and when they heard the shouts of those on board that women were to be saved first, they covered themselves with their shawls, leading the crew to believe they were women. In the darkness they escaped detection. It was not known they were Chinese until they were taken on board the Carpathia.

When it was discovered that the six Chinese had taken the places of women in the boats, some of the Carpathia's crew wanted to toss them into the sea.

It was said to-day but the officers of the Cunard vessel put them in irons Instead.

How the Chinese escaped being discovered by the crew of the Titanic or some of her passengers puzzled those on board the Carpathia.

SWINGS HIS FIST ON REPORTER'S EAR

Willie Carter Resents Question as to How He Got Into Lifeboat.

(Special to The Times-Dispatch.]

Philadelphia, Pa., April 19, 1912 --- In contrast with the attitude of many of the survivors of the Titanic, the conduct of Mrs. Willie Carter was most commented upon by those who witnessed the scenes about the Cunard pier when the Carpathia docked.

While many of the victims of the disaster roved wild-eyed about the pier the Carters exhibited no traces of the ordeal encountered on the Titanic. Mrs. Carter is well known to Philadelphia society, where she achieved fame by appearing at the Bellevue-Stratford Hotel in a split gown .showing green silk tights.

"Everyone was most kind," she said. "It was all so easy, too. Just into one boat a few hours and transferred to the Carpathia. My husband had no difficulty in getting aboard the same boat with me."

Mr. Carter was asked how he was able to get in the boat, and became very angry. Turning to the reporter, he shouted: "Repeat that question."

The reporter did and Mr. Carter, in answer, swung his right fist behind the reporter's ear, knocking him down.

Before bystanders could interfere he jumped into a waiting taxi and was whirled away.

WORLD RICHER BY GREAT DISASTER

New York World
Wreck of Titanic Shows Fine Example of Nobility and Heroism.

The- tragic disaster of the steamer Titanic was the theme of a very moving sermon by Rabbi E. N. Calisch, of the Beth Ahabah Temple, last night. He chose his text, he began, not for condemnation, but for consolation of the bereaved, and it was from the standpoint of divine providence that the disaster was treated. While taking pains to lay no blame upon particular persons, leaving that for official investigation; he said, he did ask some very pertinent questions in regard to the life-saving apparatus provided for the passengers on the Titanic.

"Why were millions lavished upon appurtenances of luxury, and beggarly hundreds denied for emergencies he stated as one of the questions which should be uppermost in the public mind. The reason why this terrible thing should have taken place was one that could not be entirely answered from the human standpoint, he added.

In conclusion, he said: "The world will be richer by this disaster – not richer in the commercial sense, but richer by reason of the fine examples of nobility and heroism offered by the men and women on board the sinking vessel." His sermon, eloquently delivered, produced a profound sensation upon his hearers.

SECTION FIVE
MAIN POINTS IN SENATE TITANIC REPORT

The Washington Times May 28, 1912

BLAMED.

Captain Smith, commanding the *Titanic*

For ignoring repeated ice warnings, without decreasing speed, doubling lookouts, and warning passengers following collision.

Capt. Stanley Lord, of the *Californian*

-For ignoring distress rockets, for "indifference or gross carelessness" when less than nineteen miles from sinking *Titanic.*

Titanic's Officers

For failure to notify passengers of danger; to load lifeboats to capacity, and to maintain discipline.

British Board of Trade

For cursory tests and inspection of new ship, lax life-saving regulations, obsolete maritime laws, and antiquated rules.

White Star Line

For suppressing news sixteen hours, and sending misleading messages.

Survivors of Crew

For failure to "bunch" survivors, and return to drowning persons.

PRAISED.

Captain Rostron, of the *Carpathia:* "For following a course deserving of the highest praise and worthy of especial recognition" in his work of commanding the rescue of the *Titanic* passengers.

SENATOR SMITH URGES CHANGE IN LAWS

Drastic Reforms Necessary to Prevent Similar Disasters on Sea.

With rare force and eloquence, Senator William Alden Smith of Michigan, chairman of the subcommittee of investigation, presented the report on the sinking of the *Titanic* on the floor of the Senate this afternoon.

Those responsible for the loss of hundreds of lives were arraigned in scathing terms for the needless sacrifice, while high tribute was paid to the courage of the heroic men, whose deeds have become known.

Cowardice and criminal inefficiency were keenly portrayed, and recommendations offered which, if carried out, will make the recurrence of such a gigantic disaster at sea impossible.

The report was accompanied by a speech of the chairman.

Brings Tears to Many.

The address of Senator Smith, at once a severe denunciation of the White Star line, a caustic criticism of the British board of trade, and its laxity of regulation under ancient and inadequate shipping laws, and a sad and mournful eulogy of the noble men and women who were plunged to their ocean graves on that fateful Sunday night, not soon to be forgotten in marine annals.

A gold medal and the thanks of Congress carrying with it the rare privilege of admission to the floor, was recommended by Senator Smith as a fitting recognition on the part of this nation, of the bravery of Captain Rostron, of the *Carpathia.*

Smith introduced a resolution to this effect at the conclusion of his speech. The measure eulogized the commander in glowing terms for the rescue of 706 of the Titanic survivors, and specified that President Taft be authorized to have struck and presented to Rostron a medal containing $1,000 worth of gold.

The resolution was adopted unanimously. In anticipation of the report and the address, a large crowd of spectators filled the galleries, and there were many wet eyes as the Senator from Michigan told, in striking fashion, the succinct and moving story of the Titanic's loss.

Overconfidence and neglect of the warnings given him faults in part expiated by the heroism of his death, were charged to Captain Smith, the commander of the Ill-fated vessel. For J. Bruce Ismay, Senator Smith had only implied criticism to make. He did not judge in specific terms of the conduct of Ismay in quitting the ship and leaving the great bulk of those on board to go down. For some of the junior officers who quickly deserted the ship he had severe criticism to offer.

Captain Lord, of the *Californian*, who was within easy reach of the *Titanic*, who was warned of the fact the *Titanic* had struck, but who yet failed to go to the rescue, came in for much condemnation. Senator Smith declared Lord has a "tremendous responsibility" placed on him which it would be difficult for him to escape.

Praise for Wireless Men.

For the gallant operators of the wireless, for Captain Rostron, of the *Carpathia*, Senator Smith had the highest praise. He spoke in especially warm terms of the conduct of Operator Phillips, of the Titanic, who paused in the chaos about him long enough to give a cup of water to a fainting woman.

On the White Star line, for sending this magnificent ship to sea with an untrained and undisciplined crew, a crew that did not know what to do when the crisis came, the Michigan Senator placed a heavy load of responsibility.

He called for such regulation of the wireless as would "clear the sea of its conflicting idioms." He reflected on the White Star Company sharply for the manner in which .false and misleading information about the disaster was given to the public on the tragic Monday following the sinking.

In striking fashion, Senator Smith thus emphasized the lack of discipline, the unpreparedness of the *Titanic* and her-crew for the terrible situation that followed on the crash into the Iceberg:

At 10 o'clock on that fateful Sunday evening this latest maritime creation was cutting Its first pathway through the North Atlantic Ocean with scarcely a ripple to retard Its progress.

Assurance of Strength

"From the builders' hands she was plunged straightway to her fate, and christening salvos acclaimed at once her birth and death. Builders of renown had launched her on the billows with confident assurance of her strength, while every port rang with praise for their achievement; shipbuilding to them was both a science and a religion; parent ships and sister ships had easily withstood the waves, while the mark of their hammer was all that was needed to give assurance of the high quality of the work.

"In the construction of the *Titanic* no limit of cost circumscribed their endeavor, and when this vessel took its place at the head of the line every modern improvement in shipbuilding was supposed to have been realized; so confident were they that both owner and builder were eager to go upon the trial trip; no sufficient tests were made of boilers or bulkheads or gearing or equipment, and no life-saving or signal devices were reviewed; officers and crew were strangers to one another and Passengers to both: neither was familiar with the vessel or its implements- for tools; no arm or station practice or helpful discipline disturbed the tranquility of that voyage, and when the crisis came a state of absolute unpreparedness stupefied both passengers and crew, and in their despair the ship went- down, carrying as needless a sacrifice of noble women and brave men as ever clustered about the judgment seat In any single moment of passing time."

For the British board of trade and its outworn and inadequate regulations, Senator Smith had this to say:

"We shall leave to the honest judgment of England its painstaking chastisement of the British board of trade, to whose laxity of regulation and hasty Inspection the world is largely indebted for this awful fatality. Of contributing causes there were very many. In the face of warning signals, speed was increased and messages of danger seemed to stimulate her to action rather than to persuade her to fear."

And in the same connection, he made this observation:

"The lessons of this hour are indeed, fruitless and its precepts ill-conceived if rules of action do not follow hard upon the day of reckoning. Obsolete and antiquated shipping laws should no longer encumber the parliamentary records of any government, and overripe administrative boards should be pruned of dead branches and less sterile precepts taught and applied."

Wants Adequate Legislation

Calling for adequate legislation that would prevent such losses as this, Senator Smith said:

"Regulation of steamship transportation is as necessary as regulation of railroad transportation and less difficult to obtain. Transportation by rail is conducted through settled localities, where many residents would quickly discover and immediately report any irregularities or disregard of safety requirements, while by water it is conducted beyond the criticism of any except the actual passengers on the ship, making it all the more necessary for definite regulations.

"Lanes of travel must be more carefully defined, strength of bow more positive and watertight subdivision to limit submergence, life-saving equipment better and numerous enough for all, discipline and practice a rudimentary exaction, eye more keen and ear alert to catch the warning cry, as on British battleships as well as on our own, powerful lights should be provided for merchant vessels to search out the partially submerged derelict; buoys should be carried by every ship to mark temporarily the place of the ship's burial in case of accident; and men of strength and spirit there must be, won back to a calling already demoralized and decadent.

"But 10 per cent of the men before the mast In our merchant marine are natives or naturalized Americans; even England, that, twenty years ago had barely 7,000 Orientals on her merchant ships,- now carries over 70,000 of that alien race. Americans must re-enlist in this service, they must become the soldiers of the sea, and, whether on lookout, on deck, or at the wheel, whether able or common seamen, they should be better paid for their labor and more highly honored in their calling; their rights must be respected, and their work carefully performed; harsh and severe restraining statutes must be repealed, and a new dignity given this Important field of labor."

RECOMMENDATIONS

That no vessel be licensed to carry passengers from United States ports until all regulations and requirements of the United States laws have been fully complied with.

That statutes be amended as to definitely require sufficient lifeboats to accommodate every passenger and every member of the crew of passenger boats.

That passengers and crew members be assigned to lifeboats before sailing.

That every ocean steamship carrying 100 or more passengers be required to carry two electric searchlights.

That a wireless operator be on duty on steamships at all hours, and that auxiliary power, either storage battery or oil engine, be required.

That all ocean and coastwise seagoing ships carrying 100 or more passengers have bulkheads so spaced that any two adjacent compartments may be flooded without sinking the vessel; that all water-tight bulkheads and decks be proportioned to withstand, without permanent deflection, a water pressure equal to five feet more than the full height of the bulkhead.

BRUCE ISMAY QUESTIONED BY SENATE
COMMITTEE

Lifeboats were rather poor affairs, and not to be depended on. Regarding the conduct of the people on the boat deck, of the port side of which he was in charge, Lightoller testified that "they could not have been quieter had they been in church."

The investigation is proceeding slowly, which is largely due to the evident lack of familiarity of the chairman, Senator Smith, of Michigan, with things nautical. To forestall this very contingency, the President placed at the disposal of the committee General Uhler, chief of the Steamboat Inspection Service, but thus far the committee has not availed itself of his services to any considerable extent. Were he permitted to interrogate the witnesses under the supervision of the committee the investigation would move much more rapidly, and the interrogator and the witness would be much less frequently at cross purposes.

In the course of his testimony Mr. Ismay said that the engines of the Titanic were making only seventy-five revolutions, while the full speed would have been eighty. This statement was partially contradicted by the second officer, who expressed the belief that the Titanic was making 22 1/2 to 23 knots when she struck the iceberg and that she could hardly have made a greater speed until she had been shaken down, meaning until use had so smoothed her bearings as to reduce the friction.

HAD SIGHTED NO ICE TWO HOURS BEFORE IMPACT.

Lightoller testified that he and learned from the captain of the proximity of ice, although none had been seen. This was from the wireless relayed from the Amerika by the Titanic. Lightoller went on watch at 6 p. m. Sunday, About 9 p. m. Captain Smith came on the bridge, discussed the possibility of meeting ice, and remarked that it was exceptionally clear, but that should it become hazy it would be necessary to reduce speed.

The captain expressed the belief that they might sight ice about 11 p. m., although the latitude of the berg sighted by the Amerika was not given, according to the witness. He believed the ship continued it full speed, although the captain might have ordered the chief engineer to reduce the number of revolutions without advising the second officer.

In this relation it is noteworthy that Captain Rostron of the Carpathia although reluctant to say anything which might be construed as a criticism of Captain Smith, was compelled to admit on examination that while he ran at full speed to the rescue of the Titanic, he doubled his lookout, and. further, that he would not, having been advised of the proximity of the ice, have taken that risk had it not been for his realization of the peril of the human complement of the Titanic, his last advices fi om that ship having been that her engine room was fast filling.

The second officer of the Titanic admitted that the precaution of doubling the lookout on his ship had not been taken. He said that Captain Smith thought his ship would be in the vicinity of the ice about 1 p. m. At 10 p.

m. Lightoller completed his watch and turned the bridge over to First Officer Murdock, who went down with the ship.

The testimony of Lightoller also served to emphasize the utter inadequacy of the lifeboat provision. There were, in all. twenty of these sixteen regulation wooden boats, two collapsible part-canvas boats and two smaller boats, which he termed "emergencies." One of the collapsibles became entangled in the tackle and was not launched at all and another, which had been stowed on top of the officers' quarters, proved so inaccessible and required so much effort to launch that it had not been put over the side when the ship went down. It then capsized, but about thirty, mostly of the crew, including Lightoller, managed to scramble on its bottom, and were subsequently taken aboard one of the lifeboats.

It was a thrilling story that was told by Captain Rostron of the Carpathia, despite the fact that he had not seen the Titanic go down, and the committee room seemed to take on the very air of the sea.

"I love a man like that," remarked one elderly spectator. "I could lick the salt off the face of such a hero."

And when, his voice faltering, the captain explained that he had not taken from one of the boats the corpse of a sailor who had perished of exposure because of the already agonized frame of mind of the survivors, and related other details of the sufferings of those who, scantily clad, had been four hours exposed to a temperature of 31 degrees, it would have been possible to hear a pin drop in the committee room.

Hardly less dramatic was the testimony of Lightoller, although at no time was he permitted to tell his story in narrative form, being subjected to constant questioning. He is a slight, determined looking young man, with clean cut features and evident simplicity, actuated by an almost painful desire to tell the exact truth, answering every question concisely and with never a suggestion of a smile, even when the chairman showed that he had supposed the "bulkheads' which were to have made the Titanic unsinkable consisted of air and watertight chambers, in which, he suggested, many of the passengers might have taken refuge on the assumption that they, at least, would float.

DIDN'T LEAVE SHIP TILL IT LEFT HIM, HE SAYS

"What time did you leave the ship?" asked Senator Smith, soon after Lightoller took the stand.

"I didn't leave it," replied Lightoller.

"Did it leave you?"

"Yes, sir."

"Was the suction a deterrent in making progress from the scene?"

"It was hardly noticeable.

"Where were you when the Titanic sank?"

"In the officers' quarters."

"Were all the lifeboats gone then?"

"All but one," said Lightoller. "I was about fifteen feet from it.

It was hanging in the tackle, and they were trying to get it over the bulwarks the last time I saw it. The first officer, Mr. Murdock. Who lost his life, was managing the tackle."

"Did you see Mr. Ismay then?"

"No."

"When did you see him?"

"When we started to uncover the boats. He was standing on the boat deck."

"What was he doing?"

"Standing still."

"Talking with any one?"

"No."

"Was he fully dressed?"

"I couldn't say for sure; it was dark."

"How long did you see Ismay there above?"

"Just as I passed."

"When you saw Mr. Ismay twenty minutes after the collision were there any other passengers near him?"

"I did not see any one in particular," said Lightoller, "but there might have been some."

A few minutes after the impact, Lightoller said, he went back to his berth.

"Why?" asked Senator Smith, in astonishment.

"Because there seemed no call for me on deck."

"Call or cause?"

"Neither call nor cause."

DESCRIBES IMPACT AS "A SLIGHT JAR."

The witness described the impact as a "slight jar followed by a grinding sound."

"You say that Sunday you were advised by the captain, by word of mouth, of icebergs in near proximity, and when you were relieved at 10 p. m., as officer of the ship, by First Officer Murdock. you passed the information to him, and he said, 'AH right'?"

"Yet-, sir."

The ship, was making about 21 to 21 knots, Lightoller testified.

According to the second officer, one hundred or more persons thrown into the water or jumped before the Titanic went down and for a few minutes they struggled, then most of them disappeared.

"The forward funnel went by the board and struck a great of those in the water," said Lightoller.

"Were any killed?"

I don't know."

A moment before the funnel broke the collapsible lifeboat, the officers' quarters floated off, and twenty or more people including Colonel Gracie. J. B. Thayer, Phillips and McBride, the wireless operators, and Lightoller, clung to the collapsed lifeboat.

The funnel hit a number of those clinging to this boat. They released their hold and sank back into the sea. The force of the funnel's forced the frail lifeboat fifty feet away from the Titanic, and left some clinging to it again struggling in the sea. Some managed to swim to the lifeboat again, but many of the unfortunates went down in the attempt, completely exhausted. Ultimately thirty persons climbed on the capsized boat.

"The lifeboats could carry sixty-five persons at risk to all, explained Lightoller, "but for safety twenty-four women and two men only were sent in the first boat."

"How did you choose seamen?"

"Those standing nearest."

"Did they want to go?"

PASSENGERS AIDED IN GETTING BOAT CLEAR.

"I didn't ask them. When we cleared the second boat I realized the situation was getting serious and put all the women nearby in it, about thirty-five. It took fifteen to twenty minutes to clear the boats and lower them with people. The boats were safe for 70 persons, provided the tackle worked right. In the third boat was only one seaman to man it. I could not spare either of the two seamen who were assisting me. A first class passenger nearby interposed and said: "I'll go, if you like."

" Are you a sailor?" I asked him. He answered: "I'm a yachtsman"

"Prove that you are a sailor by getting that fall clear. You have to be a sailor to do it," I warned him.

"He proved a good sailor, went in the boat and did brave work in protecting the women and children."

"Who was he?"

"Major Peuchen, of Toronto."

The second officer said all the women and children he could into each boat were sent away rapidly thereafter. He didn't have to count each boatload, but gathered a load for each boat.

"Were the passengers, particularly the women and children, easy to manage and quiet?"

"Yes; they couldn't have stood more quiet had they been in church."

"Where did you last see Captain Smith?" the Senator asked.

Lightoller said he saw him several times on the boat deck, but that last recollection of Captain Smith was walking across the bridge of the Titanic.

"I was busy at my own work, about fifty feet away, and I recollect seeing the captain walking across the bridge. I did not then hear him giving any ore

I was too far away.'

"When the Titanic sank were her decks intact?"

"Absolutely intact," said Lightoller.

Senator Smith asked what was the last order he heard Captain Smith give.

"When I asked if I should put the women and children in boats," replied Lightoller, "he responded, 'Yes, and lower away.' "

"What did you do?"

"Obeyed orders."

Captain A. H. Rostron of the *Carpathia* read to the committee the report he sent to the home office of the company under date of yesterday, in where he gave the details of his arrangements to cope with the situation when his vessel came up to the *Titanic*. This report is in full as follows:

"*R. M. S. Carpathia*. April 19. 1912.

"To General Manager. Cunard Steamship Company, Ltd., Liverpool.

"Sir: The following may be of interest to you. Monday, 15th inst., information: urgent distress message from *Titanic*. **Had struck ice. Require immediate assistance. Position of Titanic, 41:16 North, 50:14 West.**

I immediately ordered my ship turned and set course, we then being South 52 E. (true), fifty-eight miles from *Titanic*. Sent for chief engineer and ordered out another watch stokers and to make all possible speed. Gave orders to get all lifeboats prepared, spare gear taken out and boats swung out ready for lowering. I sent for English doctor, purser and chief steward, and gave following instructions:

"English doctor, with assistants, to remain in first class dining room.

"Italian doctor, with assistants, to remain in second class dining room.

"Hungarian doctor? With assistants, to remain in third class dining root

"Each doctor to have supplies of restoratives, stimulants and everything on hand for immediate need of probable wounded or sick.

"Purser: With assistant purser and chief steward, to receive passengers, at different gangways, controlling our own stewards and assisting passengers to dining rooms, etc. Also to get Christian names and surnames of survivors as soon as possible to send by wireless. Inspector, stewards a master-at-arms to control our own steerage passengers and keep them out of third class dining hall, and also keep them out of the way and off the deck to prevent confusion.

INSTRUCTIONS TO CARE FOR SURVIVORS.

"Chief stewards: That all hands would be called, and to have coffee ready to serve out to all our crew. Have coffee, tea, soup, etc.. in each salon, blankets in the saloons, at the gangways, and some of the boats. To see rescued cared for and immediate wants attended to.

"My cabin, and all official cabins, to be given up. Smoke room, library, dining rooms would be utilized to accommodate the survivors. All spare beds in steerage to be utilized for Titanic's passengers. All our own steerage passengers grouped together.

"Stewards should be placed in galley way, to reassure our own passengers, should they inquire about noise in getting our own boats out, etc., or the working of the engines.

"To all I strictly enjoined the necessity for order, discipline and quiet needed and to avoid all confusion.

"Chief and first officers: All the hands to be called. Get coffee, etc. Prepare and swing out all boats. All gangway doors to be opened, electric lights in each gangway and over each side. A block with line rope in each gangway. A chair slung at each gangway for getting up sick and wounded. Bo 'sun chairs, pilot ladders and canvas ash bags for children. Cargo falls, bow lines in the ends and bights secured along ship's side for boat ropes or to help the people up. Heaving lines distributed along the ship's side and gaskets handy near gangways for lashing people in chairs, etc. Forward derricks topped and rigged, and steam on winches; also told of officers for different stations and for certain eventualities.

"Ordered company's rockets to be fired at 2:45 a. m. and every quarter hour thereafter to reassure Titanic.

"I may state that canvas ash bags, were of great assistance in getting the infants and children aboard.

"I am proud and happy to state that the utmost loyalty, obedience and attention were shown to me by all the officials and the men working under them also, all working with perfect willingness and without the slightest confusion or unnecessary noises.

"As each official saw everything in readiness he reported to me personally on the bridge that all my orders were carried out, enumerating the same, and that everything was in readiness.

"The details I left to the several officials, and must say they were most efficiently carried out.

"I think you will hear from other sources that we had made every preparation possible. A. H. ROSTRON, Captain, *Carpathia*."

The night session of the Senate committee began at 9 o'clock. J. Bruce Ismay and P. A. S. Franklin, vice-president of the White Star Line, came early and took seats together in the corner behind the witness chair, where they could hear the testimony.

CARPATHIA'S OPERATOR HEARS CALL FOR HELP.

The first witness was Thomas Cottan a pink cheeked Englishman of twenty-one, who was the Marconi operator on the *Carpathia*. The *Carpathian* wireless range, he said, was about 250 miles. Conditions Sunday night were good. He had been receiving news from Cape Cod and was trying to get in touch with the *Parisian* to confirm a message previously received from her.

"I was getting ready to turn in: it was about 11," he said, "but I still had the receiver on my head. I had had a message from the *Titanic* about 5:30. It was a message for Mrs. Marshall, one of our passengers.

"I called the *Titanic*, saying I had received messages from Cape Cod for her. The reply was, 'Come at once; it is a distress message; C Q D.' I confirmed it asking them if I was to report to the captain. They answered "Yes."

"Have you been misled by messages **without** confirmation?" asked Senator Smith.

"No sir."

"Suppose this had not been confirmed?"

I would have reported it to the captain."

"Then." said Cottan, resuming his story. "I asked the *Titanic* for her position and reported it to the captain. About four minutes later I called again confirming the position, and got the answer, "All right" I heard a message from another ship calling the *Titanic*. It was the *Frankfort*, a German boat. Then I heard the *Olympic* calling the *Titanic*. The Olympic was offering her services in a message.'

"I asked the *Titanic* if they knew the *Olympic* was calling. They answered no; they could not read it because of the rush of air and the escape of steam. Then the *Titanic* called the *Olympic*, saying to come at once as they were going down. The *Olympic* acknowledged the receipt of the massage.

"Then I caught a message from the *Baltic* and told the *Titanic* to call her. I was in regular communication with the Titanic until I got the last message.

"Come quick; our engine room is filling up to the boilers." I acknowledged with the signal 'R E.' and reported to the captain.

"Then I told the *Titanic* we were coming as hard as we could can with double watch in the engine room and our boats all ready, and to be ready with the lifeboats when we came. I got no acknowledgment from the *Titanic*. I never heard from her again."

Senator Smith then began to question Cottan about conditions aboard the *Carpathia* after picking up the Titanic's survivors. He said he was on duty all day Monday, all Monday night, all day Tuesday and finally fell asleep for two or three hours Tuesday night. He said he awoke about dawn on Wednesday and was at his post all day Wednesday. On Wednesday night the junior man on the *Titanic* came up to give him a hand.

"I was rather tired, sir," said Cottan.

"Were there many attempts to communicate with your ship on Monday, Did you take any messages on Monday?"

"I can't remember what I did. The record of messages received is on file o

the ship. We were in communication with some ship all the way."

"Do you recall receiving any message from the President of the United States?"

"No, sir. The *Chester* called about 9:30 Tuesday morning for a list of the first and second class passengers. The list had been sent to the Olympic and a list of the crew and steerage had been sent to the *Minnewaska* so we did not duplicate them."

Cottan was excused with the direction to be on hand at 10 o'clock this morning- with the junior operator from the *Titanic*.

SAW MRS. STRAUS PUSH MAID INTO BOAT.

Alfred Crawford came next. He was a bedroom steward on the Titanic

He stood at the boat in which Mrs. Isidor Straus refused to embark.

"She put her foot on the gunwale," said Crawford; "then she changed her mind and went back to her husband, saying, 'We've been living together for a good many years, and where you go I go." Then she pushed her maid into the boat and stood by Mr. Straus. That was boat No. 8. The captain was personally superintending the loading of that boat. He told us to pull for a light that when we saw the light of a ship in the distance to land the women and return. We pulled and pulled, but we couldn't reach the light."

"Did you hear an explosion?" asked Senator Smith.

"I heard a sharp explosion while we were lying-to in the lifeboat. We were some distance off when she went down bow first. The lights in the bow went out first. She was clear of the water from amidships aft."

"Did you know Mr. Ismay?"

"Yes, sir."

"Did you see him?"

"Yes: he and Mr. Murdock (the first officer) were lowering No. 5, on the starboard side, under the bridge. I think it was the third boat in the water. Then I went to the other side and didn't see him get into a boat."

"They had a drill at quarters at Belfast before they sailed," Crawford said.

Crawford, too, was told to return this morning. The hearing will continue at 10 o'clock. It was adjourned about 10:30.

Senator Smith said that he adjourned somewhat earlier than he had intended because he was tired. Mr. Burlingham, secretary of the White Star Line, called his attention to the fact that many of the 210 survivors of the crew expected to sail to-day on the Lapland.

"I have no intention of holding them," said Senator Smith, "though I cannot say that I may not want some of them. I wish only to be sure that the fifteen I have subpoenaed and those who have already testified will be here."

P. A. S. Franklin joined Mr. Burlingham in assuring Senator Smith that they would be on hand.

The grand staircase on the Titanic

BLOWN FROM SHIP'S DECK

Titanic's Barber Tells of Falling on Chairs and Floating.
PICKED UP BY LIFE RAFT

Others Clinging to Its Edges Soon Became Exhausted, Said "Goodbye!" and Sank.

Special message to *The Tribune*.

Philadelphia, April l9.-August H. Welkman of Palmyra, the ship's barber on the Titanic, who was among those rescued, graphically told to-day his experience when the Titanic was lost.

Welkman who declared he has crossed the greatest times, is fifty-six years old, and for the last thirty-four years he has been employed as a ships barber by the White Star Line.

According to Welkman, he was the last man of those rescued who spoke to Colonel John Jacob Astor.

Welkman says he is a witness of the scene when J. Bruce Ismay left the Titanic, and declared that Mr. Ismay literally was thrown into the lifeboat by a seaman, who did not recognize him, and thought he was interfering with the work. He asserts that Mr. Ismay was striving to help in the work of launching the boats, and went overboard only under physical compulsion by the seamen.

"I was in my barber shop reading," said Welkman, "When I felt a slight jar and realized that we had struck something. I went to the gymnasium to see whether others had felt it. I found some of tile men punching the bag with Colonel Astor, Mr. Widener and a number of others watching them.

"I had known Mr. Widener for some time, and I advised to him to put on a lifebelt. He laughed at me. What sense is there in that: This boat isn't going to sink, he said to me. There is plenty of time. We're safer here than in a small boat, anyway.

"Then came the order to man the boats and I went on deck to help. The rule was observed of sending over four women and then a man to look after them. When four women had been put over a seaman turned to Mr. Ismay and ordered him over the side. Mr. Ismay refused to go, when the seaman seized him, rushed him to the rail and hurled him over.

"While | was still helping at the boat when there was an explosion from below decks and the ship took an awful lunge, throwing everybody into a heap. I was hurled clear of the vessel's railing and landed on top of a bundle of deck chairs which was floating on the water. I was badly bruised and my back was sprained. My Watch stopped at 1:10 a m. and I believe It was at that time I was thrown Into the water.

"While I lay floating on the bundle of chairs there came another terrific explosion and the ship seemed to split in two. There was a rain of wreckage and a big piece of timber fell on me, striking my lifebelt. I believe If It had not been for the belt I would have been killed. I floated for what I believe wan about two hours. Then an arm reached down and drew me aboard a life raft. The man who did this was a seaman named Brown, whose life I probably had saved two years ago by hurrying him to a hospital in England when he was taken ill suddenly.

"There were six persons on the raft and others were in the water up to their necks, hanging on to the edge of the raft. The raft was already awash, and we could not take them aboard. One by one as they became chilled through, they bade us goodbye and sank. In the bottom of the raft was a man whom I had shaved that morning, and whom I had been told was worth $13.000.000. I did not know his name. He was dead.

"And on we floated on the raft bereft of hope and stupefied by the calamity, until picked up by the *Carpathia* I was so badly injured they ha/I to take me on board In a boatswain's chair."

SUNDAY'S NEW-YORK TRIBUNE

LOOKING FOR SURVIVORS

St. Vincent's Hospital Alone Has One Hundred Sufferers.

MRS. A. BELMONT, VISITOR

The Financier's Wife Providing Clothes and Money for Those Left Destitute.

The hospitals of this city are treating survivors of the White Star liner Titanic with more than one hundred of them being at St. Vincent's Hospital. While others are located throughout the city.

Hundreds of persons all at the different institutions asking for relatives, seeking their friends from whom they had not heard, and listening to news of the sea tragedy from those who had been on the *Titanic* when she struck the iceberg.

The house surgeon at St. Vincent's said that nearly one- hundred patients are being treated, only three or whom aren't in favorable condition. Thirty-five of the patients are men, three of whom were of the *Titanic*'s crew. Their names are John Thompson, stoker, with a fractured right arm and William McIntyre continue with both feet frostbitten, and Thomas Whitley, waiter, burned; in fractured right leg. At Bellevue Hospital there more *Titanic* survivors; three women and four children. They were removed to the hospital early yesterday morning. Two of the children are suffering from measles, and were later taken to the Willard Parker Hospital for treatment. The women are all suffering from shock and exposure.

There are twelve women survivors at the Junior League Home, but none of them was in a serious condition, it was said. St. Luke's Hospital shelters eight survivors, four women and four children. All are suffering from exposure. Two of the women lost their husbands in the disaster.

In the Clara Home for Immigrants, survivors are being treated. One of them, Mrs. Agnes Davis, a widow, was coming from her home in Cornwall, England, to join her son in Michigan. When the *Titanic* went down Mrs. Davis was forced to leave one son. twenty years old, behind on the upper deck, while she took a younger son, only eight years old, in the lifeboat with her.

The Sydenham **Hospital**, on 16th Street, had two women patients, who were taken there last night from the *Carpathia* but left yesterday morning after being treated by the surgeons. They were Mrs. Jordan of No. 27 West 145th street and Mrs. Alma Bailey, of London, and both went to Mrs. Jordan's house.

Although the Mount Sinai Hospital housed two women patients, all information except their names was refused by those in charge. Neither is in serious condition.

Mrs. August Belmont and with women friends went to St. Vincent's yesterday and talked with many of the *Titanic* survivors. It was announced after her departure that Mrs. Belmont had arranged to make the patients comfortable with supplies of clothing und money, and would see that they were well cared for when they leave the Institution.

Mrs. Katherine Young, who. with her children. Mary, one year old. and Michael four years old, was at Bellevue Hospital, gave an account of the sinking of the Titanic yesterday. She said that after she had been placed In a lifeboat with her children, she dropped her boy into the water accidentally and thought he was drowned. Several hours later, when the *Carpathia* began picking up the Titanic's lifeboats, Mrs. Young found that Michael had been rescued by a steward in another lifeboat.

Survivors Tell Thrilling Stories of the Fearful Sea Tragedy.

SAW OFFICER SHOOT HIMSELF
Mrs. Widener Says Captain Jumped Into Ocean
Survivor States Passengers Thought
Ship Safer than Lifeboats.
Telegraph to The Tribune.

Philadelphia, April 19. All except three of the Philadelphia survivors apparently are in good physical condition. The exceptions are Mrs. George D. Widener, whose husband and son were drowned; Mrs. John B. Thayer, who mourns the death of her husband, and Augustus Welkman, who was severely injured when he was blown into the ocean by the explosion of the Titanic's boilers.

The survivors tell thrilling stories of the frightful disaster.

In describing her experience, Mrs. George D. Widener said that she had seen captain Smith of the liner jump from the bridge into the sea, and that a moment previous she had seen another officer turn a revolver upon himself and send a bullet into his brain.

Saw Officer Shoot Himself.

"Mr. Widener and I had retired to our cabin for the night," she said, "when the shock of crashing into the iceberg occurred. We thought little of it and did not leave our cabin. We must have remained there an hour before becoming fearful. Then Mr. Widener went to our son Harry's room and brought him to our cabin. A short time later Harry went to the deck and hurried back and told us that we must go on deck. Mr. Widener and

Harry, a few minutes later, went on deck and aided the officers, who were then having trouble with those in the steerage. That was the last I saw of my husband or son.

"I went on deck and was put into a lifeboat. As the boat pulled away from the Titanic I saw one of the officers shoot himself In the head and a few minutes later saw Captain Smith jump from the bridge into the sea."

Mrs. Widener at her home at Elkins Park, near here.

The entire Widener family, which is among the most prominent in Philadelphia's financial and social circles, is overcome by the disaster. The family has received messages of sympathy from all parts of the world.

When Mrs. William K. Carter stepped into a lifeboat, she saw there weren't enough men to man the oars. "There was nothing else to do," she said, "so I took an oar." And as long as the boat bobbed about in the sea she bent over the oar with the strength borne of unusual courage.

Mrs. J. B. Thayer also bent her back to the oar in the lifeboat In which she was placed, and worked for hours battling with the waves, until picked up by the Carpathia

Boats Only Partly Filled.

Mrs. Thomas Potter. Jr., declared that the passengers on the Titanic had no idea the steamer was badly damaged, and had confidence in the statement that she was nonsinkable. "As a result, the first boats to leave the vessels side were hardly filled." she said.

'"There were only about ten others in the boat in which I was, which was the first to be lowered away.

"I saw Colonel and Mrs. Astor at the rail as we moved away, and they declined to be taken oft, claiming that it was safer on the big liner than in the cockle-shell, amid the floating ice. They simply would not believe that liner was any danger. At least forty more persons could have been accommodated in our boat, if they had only listened to the ship's officer Richard M. Williams, was the last to be saved from aboard the Titanic. He was in the stern of the liner when she went down, and said that the big liner broke apart in the middle, buffeted about in the ice, he was finally able to get aboard one of the rafts and was picked up by one of the boats about two hours later.

He saw John B. Thayer. Jr, who jumped overboard from the Titanic with his father, and both managed to reach the raft. The raft was upset, however, both men being dumped into the water. The elder Thayer was never seen again, but young Thayer was picked up by one of the boats and was with Williams on the Carpathia. James McCaughey, a buyer, told one of the most complete stories of the end of the Titanic owing to his tremendous strength he had been forced Into the Second lifeboat to leave the Titanic as one of the Mr. McCaughey disagrees with most of the survivors as to the time of the accident.

He places the collision as occurring earlier than at 11:00.

The collision occurred at twenty minutes to eleven and I was in my cabin. There is nothing scarier than the racing of the screw; which often occurs when a ship sticks her nose into a heavy swell, raising the stern out of water.

There was little noise or tumult.

We were warned to dress warmly and to put on lifebelts. By this time the engine had been reversed and the ship was slowing, officers and crew ran through salon counseling calmness. I dressed and stuff my money in my pockets and went on deck.

As I passed the gymnasium I saw Colonel Astor and his wife together, she was clinging to him and pleading that they should not be separated. She made him promise to get into the lifeboat with her. He attempted to calm her, declaring the accident she soon would learn would prove to be minor.

None Knew Titanic Was Sinking.

None, I believe, knew the ship was sinking. I did not realize it then, but when I got on deck I saw tons of ice toward the bow, where we had come into collision with the iceberg. Officers were on deck with drawn guns to keep back men and were ordering the women into the boats. All feared to leave the comparative safety of the solid deck for the small craft.

Women clung to me refusing to leave, they had to be torn forcibly away. On that point all the women were firm. I would not enter the boats until they said that some men at least in them to man the oars. It required courage to step into the frail looking things. They looked as if the seas would swamp them.

An officer rushed up to me and shouted in my ear that I was big enough to pull an oar. He ordered me to get into the boat, and I did. I feared to go as I did as the ship looked safer to me. I didn't t want to but I was in the second boat that left the Titanic. Including myself and the rest of the crew, there were forty-one persons in the boat. As we pulled away we could see boat after boat filled and lowered. Despite the fact that they were new and the equipment was supposed to be first-class, the blocks jammed in many Instances, throwing the boats at a dangerous angle.

As the lifeboats pulled away we could hear an officer ordering the band to play. The *Titanic* was all aglow with lights; we pulled three-quarters of a mile away and could see her settling slowly. First we saw the lights of the lower deck snuffed out, a little later the second deck darkened, and this v. is followed by darkening of the third and upper deck.

People were crowded on the decks looking for more lifeboats. Some of them were caught in the merciless swirl as the *Titanic* went to her grave and went under with her people.

The night of the accident was not foggy or cloudy. There was just the beginning of the new moon, but the North Star in the sky was shining brightly unmarred by clouds. The boats were lowered from the sides of the *Titanic* in time to escape, but there weren't enough for all.

SECTION SIX
RIGEL: THE HERO-DOG OF THE TITANIC

By Ken Rossignol
(A story for children of all ages.)

Among the many heroes of the Titanic saga is one who is little known, his name was Rigel, an English name and an unusual name for an unusual dog. Rigel was a big Newfoundland dog, which is a breed that has a coat much like a polar bear, but unlike a polar bear, a Newfoundland is black in color. Rigel's fur and hide protected him from cold water and indeed, Newfoundland's rather enjoy swimming in cold water and they even have web-feet like a duck!

I'm not making that up!

My dog is a big yellow lab and she loves to swim, even in cold water and she loves the snow and at every chance makes snow angels but I suspect she rolls on her back all the time to scratch fleas!

Rigel belonged to the First Officer of the Titanic, Mr. Murdock. Mr. Murdock was the one who was driving the great ship on that fateful evening of April 14, 1912, when the lookouts called down from the crow's nest to report ice ahead.

Not knowing that another report of ice ahead had come an hour before and was sitting in the wireless office, undelivered to the bridge, Murdock ignored the report from the lookout.

Once more, the lookout called down to the bridge to look out for ice ahead! But Mr. Murdock did not look out.

Finally, the third time the lookout hollered, look out for ice, Mr. Murdock took action and ordered the ship to steer away from a head-on crash with the huge iceberg in their path. As you know, it didn't work out too well and the ship hit the iceberg and the lucky people went into the lifeboats and the ship went down.

Now, you wouldn't want a big black dog with fleas in your lifeboat, would you?

No, but it was okay with Rigel that he didn't enter a lifeboat as he loved to swim in cold water and he swam and swam and did the dog paddle for three hours before the rescue ship, the Carpathia, arrived on the scene.

When the Carpathia arrived where the Titanic had gone down, it had made a perilous journey, speeding across the sea through iceberg-filled waters.

Capt. Rostron had ordered his ship turned to rush through the night to attempt to save the souls on the sinking Titanic. He ordered that all of the steam being used to heat the passenger cabins be turned off so that the engines would have more power, he also doubled the lookouts so his ship wouldn't collide with an iceberg. Capt. Rostron also commanded that his crew prepare large quantities of hot water, hot chocolate, soup and coffee for the cold and weary survivors of the Titanic.

The Carpathia arrived right a daybreak, and that is not when someone "breaks" the day, but when the sun comes up!

But even with the morning arriving, it was not easy to see as the mist was heavy, icebergs and floating ice islands obscured the view of the lifeboats. The Carpathia had to carefully and slowly pick its way through the sea looking for the lifeboats which were scattered across the ocean.

As the people in the lifeboats saw the Carpathia they thanked God for deliverance and began to row their boats towards their rescuers.

Finally, Capt. Rostrum believed his crew had recovered all of the lifeboats, which had all been hoisted up onto the Carpathia. The Captain was ready to issue the order to head for New York City, as that was the destination of the Titanic and all the people on board, and heck, everyone likes to go to the Big Apple!

He walked out onto the forward section of the ship, we call that the "bow" and suddenly he heard the bark of a big dog, not the bark of the small ladies' lapdogs like they had rescued from the lifeboats, those dogs with the odd names which are hard to pronounce, but this was the big booming bark of a big dog!

The Captain walked over to the starboard side of the ship, that is the right-hand side, and he looked down into the water to attempt to find where the barking was coming from!

To his surprise, he saw Rigel, who was barking and swimming in the water next to a lifeboat that the Captain didn't know was there, it was right in front of the ship. Had it not been for Rigel's barking, the

Carpathia would have run right over the lifeboat with seventy souls on board!

Why couldn't the screams of the people on the lifeboat be heard like Rigel's barking?

That was because all of the people on the lifeboat had been screaming for help all night and they were hoarse, just like they had been at Dollyworld or Silver Dollar City on the roller coaster and screaming like ninnies! But their screams couldn't be heard as nothing came out, but Rigel was their voice and his barking saved all their lives.

There were as many as five dogs saved from the Titanic and a potbelly pig and I can't tell you if anyone ate the pig, as I don't know.

A drawing of a Newfoundland dog.

About the Author

    After covering hard news for 22 years while publishing a weekly newspaper, Rossignol sold the newspaper in 2010 and has begun devoting full time to writing and is now the author of fourteen books.

    As a maritime history speaker, Rossignol enjoys meeting audiences around the world and discussing the original news stories of the sinking of the RMS Titanic and other maritime history topics.

In 2012 and 2013 Rossignol has appeared on a dozen ships in the Pacific, Atlantic and Caribbean discussing the stories of the heroes of the Titanic, the explorations of the new world voyagers, the Bermuda Triangle, the history of piracy and other maritime history topics.

Rossignol regularly appears at the Titanic Museum Attractions in Pigeon Forge, Tennessee and Branson, Missouri for book signings and to talk with visitors about the RMS Titanic.

He has appeared on Good Morning America, ABC 20/20; ABC World News Tonight and in a currently running production of Discovery Channel Investigation Motives & Murders Series, A Body in the Bay.

News coverage of Rossignol's landmark civil rights case, represented by Levine Sullivan Koch & Schulz re: United States Fourth Circuit Court of Appeals Rossignol v Voorhaar, 2003, included articles in most major news outlets, as well as a column by syndicated columnists James J. Kilpatrick.

The story of the *St. Mary's Today* newspaper is now available in ebook and paperback: The Story of THE RAG! The book includes nearly 200 editorial cartoons that appeared over the years.

A strong highway safety advocate, Rossignol also publishes the DWIHitParade.com which focuses on impaired driving and the monthly publication, The Chesapeake.

News coverage of Rossignol's DWIHitParade won an Emmy in 2012 for WJLA reporter Jay Korff and coverage of the St. Mary's Today newspaper by WUSA reporter Bruce Leshan was awarded an Emmy in 2000.

KEN ROSSIGNOL

All books are available in ebook and paperback world-wide

The Marsha & Danny Jones Thrillers:
The Privateer Clause
Return of the Sea Empress
Follow Titanic
Follow Triangle-Vanish!
Cruise Killer

The Chesapeake: Tales & Scales
The Chesapeake: Legends, Yarns &
Barnacles
The Story of The Rag
Titanic 1912
Titanic & Lusitania: Survivor Stories
Leopold & Loeb Killed Bobby Franks
Panama 1914
Chesapeake 1850
KLAN: Killing America
Bank of Crooks & Criminals
Pirate Trials: Dastardly Deeds & Last Words
Pirate Trials: Hung by the Neck Until Dead
Battle of Solomon's Island